CW00945230

DESIGN+BUILD
YOUR DREAM HOME

ELIZABETH WILHIDE

DESIGN+BUILD
YOUR DREAM HOME

PART

1

Everyone dreams of living in the perfect house, the one that suits their needs at every level. Making the dream come true, however, is another matter entirely. You can wait until that elusive, affordable ideal home turns up in the property pages or real-estate listings, you can adapt what you have as best you can – or you can take matters into your own hands and build from scratch. There is simply no better way of bridging the gap between dreams and reality.

TURNING THE
DREAM

INTO
REALITY

RIGHT: Dream houses come in all shapes and sizes. Building your own home gives you the opportunity to step out of the mainstream and achieve a result that is tailor-made to your tastes and requirements. You may wish to build an eco house (top) or opt for a high-end prefab system, such as the Huf Haus (centre). The site itself may also inspire different structural approaches (below).

More and more people around the world are opting to do just that. In the United States, more than 100,000 of new houses constructed every year are owner-built. In Europe and Australia, the trend is also long established. In Britain, self-build is the fastest growing sector of the property market, accounting for one in eight of all new houses, which is more than the total number of those constructed by commercial house-builders.

At the start, it should be said that the routes to building a home of your own are many and various. This type of one-off project is sometimes known as 'self-build', which can be a misleading if not daunting term, hinting that you need to be the kind of hardy individual who thinks nothing of digging their own foundations. In fact, there is a broad spectrum of involvement between hands-on and hands-off. A relatively small proportion of people who build their own homes actually get their hands dirty or work on site on a regular basis. Most employ the services of a range of professionals, from architects to specialist or general contractors. For some, building their own home means buying a kit or prefabricated design and adapting it to their requirements; for others, not only the design, but also the structure and materials are uniquely specified.

If there is a range of approaches to achieving the final result, there are also many different reasons why people are inspired to build their own home in the first place. Self-builders vary from young people getting their first toehold on the property ladder, to those with growing families, right through to couples of retirement age who find themselves in the position to achieve a lifelong dream. Some self-builders are committed to living green and find that building their own home is the only way to achieve a high level of sustainability. Others – and many architects and designers fall into this category – seize upon the opportunity for creative expression. But what they all have

in common is that they have encountered a mismatch between what is on offer in the housing market and the type of house in which they really want to live.

In parts of the world where the bulk of the existing housing stock dates back half a century or more, endeavouring to accommodate today's notions of light, space and function within surroundings that are many decades out of step can be costly and ultimately frustrating. Increasingly, we crave plenty of natural light; older houses, particularly in rural settings, tend to be dark, with relatively small windows. We want homes that embrace the outdoors, whereas older houses are often inward-looking. Crucially, we want the feeling of spaciousness; in many period houses, up to one-third of the floor area is devoted to staircases, landings and hallways, leaving the individual rooms relatively small in scale.

Of course, older houses can be converted or adapted, and it is true that behind many a Victorian or Edwardian façade lurks a surprisingly contemporary home. There is inevitably a limit, however, to what you can – or should – do to an existing property; major structural alterations and upgrading servicing do not come cheap. In planning and arrangement, a house dating from the nineteenth century, for example, reflects the social mores of that period, where the hierarchy of use and activity was spelled out in the provision of separate rooms, each assigned a different function, rather than open, multipurpose space that is today's preference.

When it comes to new developments, these are often no less satisfactory. Developers and commercial house-builders are notoriously conservative the world over and many 'new' houses wear period clothes, like a kind of meretricious fancy dress. Worse, a high proportion have been designed with a 'one-size-fits-all' mentality that results in no better accommodation of individual needs and tastes than a Victorian terraced house. In response

to changing lifestyles and rapid advances in technology, flexibility is what many people want from their homes, but what few commercial developers have thought to provide. The result is that buying a new home often means buying someone else's idea of what a home should be and, what is more, paying a premium for it in terms of the developer's profit.

The desire to create an environment tailor-made to one's needs is a powerful motivation. Still, self-build would not be as popular as it is if there were not other, equally compelling incentives. For many, the most persuasive of these is financial. If you do your sums right and are level-headed about budgeting, you will spend less than you would buying an equivalent existing house in the same location – in some cases between 20 and 30 per cent less. In some parts of the world where property values are skyrocketing, building your own home may be the only way of obtaining the space that you need right where you want to live.

In the past, financing a new build was a major stumbling block for many people. As the trend has accelerated, however, new financial products have come onto the market, such as self-build mortgages, which have made these kind of projects much more feasible for those who do not already have large sums sitting around in the bank. The arrival of the Internet has also smoothed the self-build path. With everything from site-finding agencies, specialist materials, structural frames, prefab and kit houses only a mouse-click away, researching alternatives has never been so straightforward. Many people who build their own homes source materials and sometimes complete structural systems from companies halfway around the globe. Connectivity has not made this possible in itself, but it has made it much faster and easier.

In terms of negotiating official hurdles, matters have also become somewhat less fraught. As more people choose to build their own homes, planners and other agencies have become more familiar with the type of issues, both stylistic and structural, that such projects raise. In Britain, for example, early proponents of timber-frame construction often found they had a fight on their hands to convince building inspectors that this type of system was capable of meeting the same standards as the more prevalent masonry construction. Green pioneers, building with adobe, straw bale or cob, had even tougher campaigns. This is not to say that any scheme that you conceive will sail through without raising objections, but there are definitely more precedents around now that can be cited to bolster your case with planners.

Many people imagine that you need to have exceptional qualities to build your own home. While it is true that you need patience and commitment, these characteristics are also required if you are attempting major building work, converting a loft or putting in a new kitchen. Building a new home is necessarily more involved and will take a lot longer, but it does not require superhuman levels of tolerance and persistence. A practical bent comes in handy and will save you money if you can tackle some of the work yourself. A good head for organization is also very useful, and project management is where many self-builders find that they excel. Perhaps the most important requirement, however, is the willingness to take the plunge in the first place.

Every building project is unique and throws up different solutions to different problems or areas of difficulty, whether it is the challenge of fitting accommodation into an awkward urban infill site, coping with the unexpected or simply keeping on budget and schedule. Meeting such challenges and overcoming them is what provides such a huge personal sense of satisfaction and achievement – rewards every bit as valuable and enduring as that of achieving the house of your dreams.

LEFT: The site is unique and so is the house, designed to take full advantage of it. Raised on stilts, like an over-scaled treehouse, this family home near San Diego provides ample decks and roof terraces from which to enjoy the spectacular setting.

URBAN

DEVELOPMENTS

ffinch street, DEPTFORD, LONDON, UK

ARCHITECT: Robert Doe

Deptford is a densely populated area of southeast London near Greenwich, where nineteenth-century terraced houses, light industrial units and multistorey estates coexist in a typical urban medley of disparate building styles and uses. This particular gap, or infill, site is squeezed between a shopping street and an industrial area, and occupies part of a designated conservation area, a factor that could have posed a number of constraints when it came to architectural style and choice of materials. Fortunately, the local planners proved open-minded and were ultimately sympathetic to a more contemporary approach. A calm and uncomplicated design is the result.

The three-storey building distinctively clad in cedar weatherboarding is carefully sited on the plot itself, set back from the street behind galvanized steel fences which offer partial screening from passing traffic, human and vehicular. The front yard has enough space for a tree and a car parking space. A yard to the side offers shared access to both units that comprise the building via an external stair to the main entrances at ground and first-floor levels. At the rear is a small private yard that serves the ground-level unit.

With the accelerating trend to work at home, it is increasingly important to provide adaptable space for living and working. This building has been designed for use either as two separate live-work units or as a single unit, with working space at the ground level and living areas on the two floors above. Internal space has been maximized by the external access stair connecting the two parts

of the building, and all habitable rooms – that is, all areas excluding bathrooms, showers and kitchens – are computer networked, to achieve a high degree of in-built flexibility of use. On the ground-floor level, the unit comprises a simple rectangular space with a single-storey extension that houses a small kitchen and shower room. The upper unit, arranged over the first and second storeys, includes a double-height south-facing room, a combined living and kitchen area. On the first floor, overlooking the front, there is a tub room and another room that can either be used as a bedroom or workspace. On the level above, tucked beneath the roof pitch, is a storeroom, along with a second bedroom or workspace. The volume of the building is cut into at the upper and lower levels to make an overhang and a balcony, respectively.

In both design and orientation, the building makes the most of natural light, with the result

ABOVE: The front elevation of the house is set well back from a busy street. Galvanized steel fencing screens the house from passing traffic. The front yard is large enough to accommodate a car parking space.

15

ABOVE: The house under construction. The basic structure is a lightweight steel frame that was locally made. External cladding is made of cedarwood. The house has been designed in accordance with many principles of environmentally responsible construction.

RIGHT: A side view clearly shows the two cutaways into the main volume, which form a balcony at the top and an overhang on the lower level. The entrances to both units are at the side.

that not only are internal spaces bright and airy, but also ongoing energy costs are reduced – a definite plus in terms of being environmentally friendly, as well as being more economical. A key factor is the siting of the main double-height living space on the south-facing aspect, where large windows and rooflights flood the interior with warm light. There are also roof-lights over the internal stairwell as well as internal windows to provide indirect natural light for the bedroom and storeroom located on the second level.

Designed to accommodate future shifts in both use and need, the building also embodies many of the principles of environmentally responsible construction. The basic structure consists of a lightweight steel frame, which was fabricated locally – 2.5km (1½ miles away) – and delivered to site for erection by hand, all of which minimized transport costs and local disturbance. Steel is a material that is high in

embodied energy, but this type of local sourcing reduces another environmental impact that is associated with its use, which is the energy costs involved in long-distance transportation. Galvanized-steel external stairs and the 'Juliet' balcony that is accessed by double doors in the living area were both simply bolted on to the steel frame. An insulated overcoat over the frame minimizes heat loss, and full-length metal roof panels drain front to back. Run-off to ground level surfaces is drained through gaps between block paviors.

The use of materials was equally informed by ecological considerations. The only external materials that will require routine maintenance are the painted timber frames to the windows and doors. The cladding, in western red cedar, was sourced from well-managed Canadian forests. As it needs no further finishing it has been left undecorated. Internal floor finishes consist of plywood boards, from a source

RIGHT: Internal windows and roof-lights fill the interior with natural light.

RIGHT: Very simple materials were used throughout the interior. The flooring is plywood in the main areas, with linoleum in the tub room. Heating is supplied by underfloor heating and there is a solar panel on the roof to provide additional hot water for the upper unit.

FAR RIGHT: The house requires very little in the way of external maintenance. The cladding has been left untreated.

certified by the Forest Stewardship Council, with linoleum, a wholly natural product, being utilized in the tub room.

The entire building has underfloor heating, run from condensing boilers. A solar panel on the roof provides supplementary hot water for the upper unit. Water-saving features include very low volume 4-litre (1-gallon) flush toilets and water-saving taps (faucets). All external and internal light fittings use low-energy compact fluorescent light bulbs.

Modest and yet uncompromising in terms of standards, this thoughtful design provides flexible accommodation on what is a relatively tight urban site. Not only is it sustainable in terms of construction, materials and energy use, but it also demonstrates how seamlessly environmental considerations can be integrated into a contemporary approach to building with no subsequent loss of useability, practicality, visual appeal or ease of living.

2

bercy residence, AUSTIN, TEXAS, USA

ARCHITECT: Bercy Chen Studio

Located in the Bouldin Creek neighbourhood of south Austin, these two beautifully refined glass-and-steel pavilions provide a home for two families and a showcase for the design talent of an architectural partnership. Thomas Bercy and Calvin Chen were recent graduates when they went into practice together; this house, their first built work, now serves as a home for Bercy and his brother Yannick, who has a young family. A bohemian enclave close to the city centre, Bouldin Creek is one of the few centrally located areas in Austin where vacant lots are still available for development. Nevertheless, it took two years of false starts before they finally found the right piece of land.

The next stage was to come up with a way to design a house for two different styles of living. After toying with the idea of subdividing a single structure, Bercy's design partner, Chen, came up with the notion of two separate pavilions. One would provide accommodation for Yannick and his family (two bedrooms and a bathroom), with the other two-storey structure being devoted to common areas – living room, kitchen and dining room – on the ground floor, and an apartment for Bercy on the upper level. A glass hallway connects the two volumes.

The site itself is narrow and the positioning of the pavilions, tight on the side boundaries, creates a dynamic central courtyard space to which both buildings are orientated. The central focus is the reflecting pool, bridged by the glass hallway. The inner walls of both pavilions are open to the water garden; walls on the boundaries are closed. The pavilions are parallel to each other but staggered, an arrangement

which creates a deck area at the front, with a more private outdoor living area at the rear.

The structural system was designed both for economy and efficiency, and is revealed in the articulation of the elevational treatments. Modular-steel frames, infilled with ThermaSteel (structural panels made of galvanized steel and a special resin which provide a vapour barrier and exceptionally high insulation ratings), were used to construct both pavilions. Given the hot Texan sun, and the expanses of glass used, this high degree of efficiency was crucial. The walls' glazed portions are 1.8m x 2.75m (6ft x 9ft) sliding doors, double-glazed and insulated, and were sourced from a specialist company. The structure of the second storey in one pavilion is a Vierendeel truss. This acts like a bridge and minimizes the need for vertical support in the floor below, thus giving clearer spaces.

One of the design's most striking aspects is the two coloured cores in each building.

ABOVE: The two pavilions that comprise the development are situated in an enclave of south Austin that is popular with creative professionals. The basic structure was a steel frame infilled with glass and structural panels. The project team included Bercy Chen associates Joseph Winkler and Bryan Dixon.

21

ABOVE: The lightness of the pavilions and the way in which they are sited with respect to each other recalls the transparency and minimalism of Japanese design.
RIGHT: Glass is used extensively. The sliding doors are double-glazed and highly insulated.

These house all the service areas – kitchen, bathrooms, utility and storage room. Grouping most of the plumbing, heating, cooling and electrical systems maximizes efficiency. Each core is boldly signalled by colour – steel stud frames are covered with 10mm (⅜in) blue or red acrylic panels backlit by fluorescent light at night to form glowing light sculptures.

The fixing of the acrylic panels posed the construction's one major headache. First, it took a while to work out a method of attaching the panels to the frame that allowed for movement of the plastic material with fluctuations of temperature – double-sided construction tape was eventually decided upon. When the panels were delivered to site, they were perfectly true; four days of exposure to hot sun later and they were rippled with warping. Although it proved possible to salvage the panels and attach them to the frames, installation costs doubled.

The Bercy brothers are Belgian, while Chen, who is Taiwanese, has lived all over the world. Naturally, the design abounds in references to other regional architectural styles and cultures. The use of flat roofs as an additional outdoor space for dining is borrowed from Moorish architecture, as is the retractable awning made of a shading tarpaulin normally used in plant nurseries. The reflecting pool and the spatial continuity between indoor and outdoor areas were inspired by Asian architecture, while the transparency and minimalism of the pavilions recall Japanese design. Ceilings and interior walls are clad in sealed cabinet-grade birch plywood to form a sleek, warm skin. Extraneous details such as doorknobs are absent. Doors are opened by means of pulls that lie flat when not in use and which are usually used on boats.

Another feature is the trellis or sunbreak shading the front patio. Made of slats of ipe, a Brazilian hardwood, it projects out in a continuous canopy over ground-floor windows, then extends up and over the second storey. Functional yet beautiful, too, this telling detail reflects the designers' success in marrying the practical with the artistic and expressive.

LEFT: The flat roof, which provides additional dining space, is a reference to Moorish architecture. It is shaded by a retractable awning, with fixings sourced from the nautical industry. The front patio is shaded by an ipe trellis which wraps up to form a canopy over the first-floor windows.

ABOVE: One of the most striking features of the pavilions is the coloured cores, where most of the servicing is grouped. The coloured acrylic panels were fixed using double-sided construction tape.

BELOW: A glass hallway connects the two pavilions. The central focus is a reflecting pool.

3

fung/blatt residence, LOS ANGELES, CALIFORNIA, USA

ARCHITECT: Fung + Blatt

Occupying a typical urban rectangle, this open, flexible house was designed as a family home for the architects and their two daughters. The site is on the north-facing slope of a shallow canyon in Mount Washington, a hilly, diverse neighbourhood near downtown Los Angeles. The entire project was informed by the desire to conserve resources and keep within a fairly tight budget. So while the site is some 465sq m (5,000sq ft), the house itself is a modest 149sq m (1,600sq ft), meeting the family's present needs while allowing for expansion and changing uses. Both the attic and the garage (which is plumbed for another bathroom) were designed with the notion of future conversion in mind.

Patios and terraces at different levels on the sloping site serve as extensions of indoor areas and multiple circulation paths enrich the sense of space. Around the exterior, the terrace on the garage roof, which serves as an extension of the living area, connects to a ground-level dining patio. From the dining patio, in turn, it is possible to climb up to the upper garden and re-enter the house. These various routes, both indoors and out, generate a feeling of expansiveness and vitality that belie the relatively small size of the house.

The house is stepped back from the street in accordance with local setback rules and is entered via a shaded garden and a small foyer. Instead of constructing patio walls the boundaries of the garden are defined by galvanized-steel planters filled with reeds and other hardy species. Sections of corrugated steel, the same used to make the roof, are staked with salvaged portions of stop-sign posts, to form retaining walls that prevent the heavy clay soil from spilling into the street during a rainstorm. To conserve water, drought-resistant species such as bamboo and cacti that require little additional irrigation – unlike the stereotypical suburban lawn – were chosen for outdoor planting.

The house is conceived as an interplay of contrasting volumes. On the ground floor, a central open stair separates living and service areas. The main living area is a soaring space 7.3m (24ft) high that extends over the garage to form an external deck; glazed doors fold back to merge indoors with out. The kitchen/dining space is tucked against the hill and expands laterally to patios that climb behind the house; the study is minimally partitioned from the living area by double-sided bookshelves that stop short of the ceiling. In the kitchen, a cabinet housing a stacked washer and dryer serves as the back wall of a guest bathroom.

ABOVE: The house is sited on a north-facing slope, set well back from the street. The curved roof, which is such a distinctive feature of the elevation, is made of corrugated steel. The basic structure is made of a steel frame and concrete blocks.

27

The ceiling height of the main space was dictated by the need to catch sunlight coming over the slope of the hill in winter. The north-facing clerestory windows allow passive cooling throughout the day during the summer. Neither of the bedrooms on the upper floor is fully enclosed. The girls' bedroom has an internal window that provides views across and down through the main space.

More radically, neither of the two bedrooms on the level above is fully enclosed, a strategy that is as much about generating a sense of inclusiveness as it is a means of facilitating cross-ventilation and maximizing light. The main bedroom opens into the living-room volume and connects via a hand-built ladder to a snug attic which will serve in future as a retreat. Although it has its own entrance from a hallway, a preferred route is via a family dressing area with double sinks and through a walk-in closet. The girls' room, which is the same size as their parents', has an internal window that provides views across to the main bedroom and down into the dining area. An open playroom leads to a grassy patch behind the house. The only fully enclosed spaces are the toilets and bathing areas.

The basic structure is an efficient modular armature of concrete and steel. To conserve resources and keep within budget, interior materials are similarly robust and forthright – concrete, steel and birch ply – employed for maximum practicality and longevity, and lightly

finished in an honest expression of material integrity. The staircase's open birch-ply treads can be simply turned over when the facing side has worn out. The small, tightly planned kitchen is fitted with cabinets made of Latvian birch ply, and has rugged concrete walls. The flooring in the living area is concrete, while galvanized steel is used to clad the fireplace.

The house is sited on a north-facing hill, which meant that the ceiling height of the main space was dictated by the need to catch light coming over the slope in winter. In summer, north-facing clerestory windows provide even light and passive cooling throughout the day, aided by canyon breezes; in the cooler months, warm air collecting under the vast ceiling and warmth retained in the concrete floor needs minimal heating to make a comfortable indoor climate. Along with the changes in ground plane which create a variety of spatial experience, the house is truly in tune with its setting.

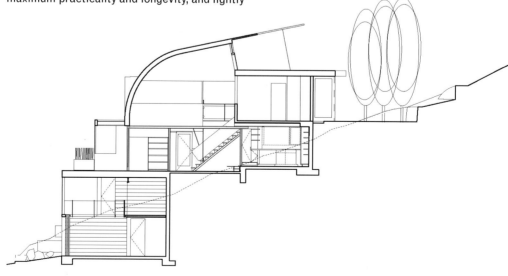

Varied routes around the house, both internally and externally, generate a feeling of expansiveness and vitality that make the house feel much bigger than it actually is.

ABOVE: The front elevation of the house is set back from the street in accordance with local rules. Drought-resistant plants in corrugated steel planters form retaining walls to prevent soil erosion during heavy rainstorms.

LEFT: Internally, materials are simple and robust, and are often left unfinished. The floor in the main living area is concrete, while galvanized steel is used to clad the fireplace.

RIGHT: The kitchen cabinets are made of Latvian birch ply.

4

redel house, WANDSWORTH, LONDON, UK

ARCHITECT: Smith Caradoc-Hodgkins

More often than not, the most difficult part of building a new house in an urban area is finding a site, particularly in popular residential locations. It always pays to keep one's eyes open. The plot on which this family house has been built is situated in an area of south London largely given over to streets of terraced Victorian houses. It was first spotted by the Redels when they were visiting friends for dinner. From that first sighting of the land to the house's completion took nearly a decade of persistence in the face of numerous setbacks and reversals – not to mention the extremely testing experience of living in two separate building sites.

It often takes vision to see the opportunity and potential inherent in urban sites. This one was no exception. It was large but derelict, with an old garage on it, and was situated at the rear of a boarded-up house. There was no planning permission for development in place and no guarantee that consent would be granted. In addition, the house's sole occupant, a squatter who was an upholsterer, was understandably reluctant to divulge the name of the owner of the house and land. Ron Redel, however, was determined and, after months of pleading, he finally persuaded the upholsterer to give him the information he needed to contact the owner.

The purchase presented another hurdle. The Redels' offer for the house and land was rejected. The house stood empty for a further two years, during which time Ron established through discussions with local planners that the type of scheme he had in mind might be acceptable. Finally, the owner agreed to sell.

The basic strategy of the development was to restore and extend the old house at the front of the site and sell it to finance a new building at the rear which would serve as a family home. Outline planning permission for the new house was awarded the year after the purchase of the site, by which time renovation work on the old existing house was under way. This proved to be a more protracted business than the Redels had expected, so to save money they moved into the incomplete renovation, making do at first with no kitchen, bathroom or floorboards.

Meanwhile the site for the new house had been cleared, the old garage demolished and a team of architects was engaged in drawing up the plans to be submitted for full planning permission. The proposed scheme, a modern concrete, glass and steel structure, included four bedrooms and a study, as well as living accommodation. At this stage, the Redels ran into yet another hitch.

ABOVE: The location of this house is at the rear of an existing property. The site was derelict and overgrown. The new structure is a modern concrete, glass and steel building that provides airy flexible space.

While UK planning law does not recognize a right to a 'view', any scheme that deprives neighbouring properties or gardens of light may be legitimately overruled. When neighbours saw the proposals for the new house, concerns grew and the scheme had to be redrafted to take into account their objections. The result was a lower roofline that sloped to prevent light to adjacent properties being blocked, and a smaller footprint to provide more space between the house and the site's boundary. The new design was for some 220sq m (2,360sq ft) of accommodation. These changes and plan resubmission took time, and approval was finally awarded three years after outline consent was granted and four years after initial purchase.

The renovation of the existing house had come to an end. Ron Redel, who had worked closely with the architects on the design and specification of the new house, decided to do without a project manager and to hire the relevant contractors for the new build himself, a decision he later regretted. Builders were engaged to construct the basic concrete-and-steel shell, which was up and roofed by the end of the year in which final approval was gained.

With the principal building works due to be finished within another month, the family went on a well-deserved holiday, only to discover on their return that no work had been carried out on site at all during their absence. The renovated house had now been sold, so they had no choice but to camp out in the new, incomplete house, which lacked kitchen, bathroom and staircase.

The surfaces and finishes chosen for the new house are of high specification, which lead to yet more difficulties. Ron had decided upon polished concrete floors for the living and dining rooms. The builders tried a total of six times to get it right, but each time the concrete failed. Eventually, the resin flooring specified for the kitchen was extended to those areas as well.

Other special features include underfloor heating, a galvanized roof and a thermal coating applied to the exterior, which makes the house exceptionally well insulated. The kitchen has solid walnut work surfaces; the bathroom flooring is bamboo.

After such a wait, the Redels' persistence has more than paid off. The amendments to their original plans, which resulted in a lower, sloping roof, has produced a sun-filled atrium that bathes the interior with light. Far from being deterred by their experiences, they are planning to do it again, to create a bigger house for their growing family.

ABOVE: A decked terrace planted with architectural plants serves as an extension of the main living space.
LEFT: After a few false starts trying to lay level concrete, resin was chosen as the flooring in the main living and dining areas.
INSET: The sloping roofline of the house was dictated by the need to prevent light from being blocked to neighbouring properties. The result, a sun-filled atrium that bathes the interior with light, proved no compromise to design and spatial quality.

35

THIS PAGE: The house has been finished to a high specification, with underfloor heating and a high degree of insulation. Folding glazed doors open to join the main living area to the decked external terrace.

5

steinhardt residence, BIRMINGHAM, MICHIGAN, USA

ARCHITECT: McIntosh Poris Associates

New York loft living was the inspiration behind the design of this contemporary urban townhouse, the home of kitchen designer Janice Steinhardt. While an architectural exhibition at New York's Museum of Modern Art in 1999 helped to confirm her ideas, she had already commissioned architects McIntosh Poris to come up with a scheme, giving them a file full of interiors and exterior images of the type of designs she liked. Manhattan may have been much on the client's mind, but the location of her home is Birmingham, Michigan, a leafy, villagey suburb of Detroit, where well-heeled Detroiters used to vacation in the eighteenth and nineteenth centuries.

Today, a large part of Birmingham's appeal is the fact that it has retained its downtown shopping district, unlike so many other small towns which have lost theirs to the ubiquitous mall. Located less than two blocks from the downtown area, the site offered Steinhardt a close approximation of that urban experience of opening your front door and finding what you need – bookstore or restaurant – within easy walking distance. Despite this, Birmingham largely presents a traditional image, and neighbouring properties, many of which date from the 1920s, are chiefly Arts and Crafts or neocolonial in style, built of brick or timber, and with steep pitched roofs. Prominent among them on its corner site, this steel-framed house with its large metal-framed windows registers as a most definite shock of the new.

The contrast of styles was not lost on local residents. As soon as the steel frame began to go up – and a photograph of construction was published in a Detroit newspaper – complaints started to roll in. The local building department received a total of 11 complaints during the construction period, some petty, but most seeming to arise out of the anxiety that a modernist house might erode the existing sense of community. While the design does make a few nods in the direction of the traditional – the front stoop, the shallow pitch of the roof and the cream-coloured block cladding – it remains unashamedly modern, which is what the client wanted.

The house covers some 325sq m (3,500sq ft) arranged over three levels – basement, ground and first floor – and includes two porches, one of which is screened, and a private terrace. Internally, it is spare and open, with minimal partitioning to break up the space. Storage is either concealed or used as spatial dividers. A central open steel staircase connects the three levels. In the basement are two guest

ABOVE: A stunning contemporary addition to a leafy Detroit suburb, this house was not without its local detractors but has since won hearts and minds. The exterior is faced in creamy block; the windows are metal-framed and the chimney is sheathed in steel.

ABOVE: The house under construction, showing the steel frame. **RIGHT:** The immediate neighbourhood features traditional-style houses, many of which date from the 1920s. The new house was inspired by contemporary designs exhibited at an architectural exhibition and by Manhattan loft-style interiors.

bedrooms that look out over a sunken terrace, as well as a bathroom and exercise room. The ground floor is more or less entirely open, fitted and furnished to support a sequence of overlapping activities, from the main living area through the dining area, to the kitchen with its own adjoining sitting area. The only walls enclose a central cube that houses a closet and toilet. Upstairs, where all walls stop short of the ceiling, a storage area separates the master bedroom and bathroom from an office that overlooks the main living area downstairs. The flow of space and lack of partitioning beyond what is strictly necessary give the entire house a loft-like feel. However, with windows on all sides – some of them double-height – the house is much lighter and airier than the average converted loft building.

Steinhardt consulted closely with the architects on the choice of materials, interior finishes and furnishings, something which resulted in a highly integrated design process. Not surprisingly, the kitchen was a particular focus of interest. As a kitchen designer who often hosts charity events for up to 100 people at home, she is well aware that the kitchen is where people naturally congregate and was determined to make it as beautiful as possible. One early stipulation was that there be no wall-hung storage – she preferred to be able to look out of windows when working in the kitchen. The solution consisted of a series of base units tucked under the long soapstone counter, as well as two built-in storage areas housing ovens, and fridges and freezers concealed behind Italian walnut cabinetry. All in all, the design is highly functional, but sleek and minimal at the same time.

Throughout the house, the materials used display a contemporary edge. The ground floor is concrete, with underfloor heating, while on the storey above, the flooring is maple. The

fireplaces have limestone surrounds. The steel staircase and aluminium-framed commercial windows have an industrial aesthetic. This modernist palette is echoed in the choice of furnishings, which includes classic pieces by Le Corbusier such as his Grand Confort armchair and chaise-longue, design icons that date back to the 1920s. On the exterior of the house, the metal deck which wraps around the building to form a terrace is suggestive of an urban fire escape, and the chimney is sheathed in steel.

Modern through and through, the house has succeeded in winning over its critics. Not only has it received architectural awards, both for its design and its integration into the neighbourhood, but it has also been added to the Birmingham House Tour – a sure sign of a local landmark in the making.

FAR LEFT: Lack of partitions, large areas of glazing and an open staircase create an airy, expansive interior.
LEFT: Dark mosaic tiling is used on the walls of the guest bathroom, which has a shower and a whirlpool tub.
BELOW LEFT: A metal deck wraps around the house to form a terrace. Large windows, some double-height, flood the interior with light.
BELOW: The kitchen is a beautifully detailed functional space with base units tucked under a long soapstone counter. The flooring throughout the main areas is concrete.

The client, a kitchen designer, consulted closely with the architects on the choice of materials, interior finishes and fittings, which resulted in a highly integrated design process.

canal house, VENICE, CALIFORNIA, USA

ARCHITECT: Sander Architects

For many people, designing and building their own home provides the perfect opportunity to try something different. Lateral thinking can throw up exciting, original and innovative ideas, whether in terms of the design itself or in the use of materials that are not generally associated with construction. Architect Whitney Sander's canalside home, office and studio is a laboratory of ideas that reflects his passion for working with materials – green materials and the products of new technologies, as well as those borrowed from other applications. The result, a sensuous modernism, is an evocative meeting of opposites.

44

With only himself to please, Sander could afford to take the time for some creative daydreaming. He spent an entire year designing the scheme and carried on sketching and improvising all the while the house was being constructed. A good starting point, he maintains, echoing Australian architect Glenn Murcutt, is 'what is necessary'; beyond the practicalities lies scope for more poetic expression.

The Canal House is sited on a narrow site only 8.5m (28ft) wide that runs between a small street and a canal, with little space to either side and no boundary fencing. The house is composed of three cubes, one raised at the street frontage to form a studio and the other two, sited on the canalside, forming the combined house and office. Although the site was tight, Sander decided to sacrifice some space to separate the house from the studio, the two volumes providing a richer sequence of spatial experience than could be delivered

by a single building. On the north and east façades, where the walls are not glazed or infilled with acrylic, exterior MDO sheathing is covered with perforated aluminium which glints in the light and dissolves the solid form of the structures.

On the street frontage, the studio, raised on fine columns over the carport, presents an open aspect, with floor-to-ceiling glass windows and acrylic panels on three sides. Horizontal steel fins mitigate the effect of strong light; at night, lit from within, the dramatically gridded façade raised on its thin stilt-like supports resembles a Japanese lantern. Reached via a spiral staircase, the studio is a pure and simple space that is ideal for creative work.

The double-cube volume of the house and office is similarly open, with floor-to-ceiling windows and vertical louvres to draw in cooling breezes. Screening the house and its small rock garden and patio from the canal

ABOVE: Folded and wrapped strips of acrylic encircle the central atrium of the house, making a translucent screen that separates sleeping and bathing areas from the office. Each fold was bent in a special mould and all the panels were sanded by hand.

traffic at the rear is a screen of fast-growing papyrus. For greater privacy at night, when the expanse of glass wall attracts the attention of passers-by on the canal path, Sander has devised drapery made of parachute nylon that can be drawn around the living area 'like a swaddling blanket'; the softness of the draped material forms a counterpart to the crisp form of the steel and glass structure.

The interior of the house and studio is open and loft-like, arranged around a central atrium that rises up 7.6m (25ft) over the ground floor. There are few partitions, which keeps the various spaces flexible for future changes of use. The main living area on the ground floor is divided into three separate zones. At the rear is the kitchen; in the middle is the dining area, with a table and base designed by Sander, and at the front, facing the canal, is a seating area, furnished with pieces designed by George Nakashima, inherited from Sander's

parents. Upstairs is a bedroom and an office connected by a gallery walkway. The office has long vertical windows that look over the studio.

While the studio is a rigorous and pure working environment, the house has a softer, more playful quality that is achieved through the contrast of hard and soft surfaces, curves and sharp angles. The flooring on ground level is polished concrete stained a dark walnut colour; on the level above, the walkway connecting bedroom to office is a softer bamboo. The stair treads, fireplace hearth and overmantel are made of folded sheets of 12mm (½in) steel plate; the kitchen island is formed of cantilevered sheets of Panelite, a composite cast polymer material. The cast resin bathroom sinks were designed expressly for the house and are now marketed by Sander Architects as a new product line.

The most evocative use of material, however, is the sensuously folded, warped and wrapped

LEFT: The house and studio under construction. The basic structure is steel-frame. The site itself is a narrow plot that runs between a street, from which the studio is accessed, and a canal. A small rock garden and patio separate house from canal.

BELOW: The cube that houses the architectural studio is raised on fine columns over a carport. Floor-to-ceiling windows and acrylic panels wrap the building on three sides, with steel fins acting as sunbreaks. On solid sides, exterior timber is clad with perforated aluminium.

FAR LEFT: The main area on the ground floor is divided into zones for living, cooking and dining. The dining area occupies the central portion of the space; the table was designed by Sander. Parachute nylon drapery provides privacy at night.

LEFT: The acrylic panels serve as screening on the upper level while allowing natural light to pass through.

BELOW: The bathroom features cast resin sinks which were designed especially for the house and are now marketed by Sander's practice.

strips of acrylic which encircle the central atrium. Described by Sander as a 'pseudo' Mobius strip, the divider begins on the upper floor as four ribbons of 60cm (2ft) high panels, forming a wall to wrap the gallery between office and bedroom, and make a translucent screen for the sleeping and bathing areas. Descending from the upper level, the panelling is then reduced to two ribbons serving as handrail and divider, before emerging on the ground floor as a single ribbon serving as a guardrail. Each corner of this sinuous strip took six hours to bend in a special mould. All the acrylic panels were sanded by hand, a labour of some 50 hours.

Both the studio and residence are filled with light – to the extent to which Sander's book bindings have become bleached. The interiors are also bursting with an innovative and expressive use of materials which injects liberal doses of wit and vitality into the experience of space. The material quality of the building is heightened by a series of contrasts: soft parachute nylon drapery contrasting with steel columns, stairs and fireplace; glass, acrylic and Panelite sheets used to make the kitchen island, contrasting with concrete flooring. It is small wonder that the project has received numerous design and architectural awards.

7

stealth house, DULWICH, LONDON, UK

ARCHITECT: Robert Dye Architects

A good match between client and architect can go a long way towards achieving a successful result. Geof Powell had long cherished a dream to build a modern house, and over the years he had collected a scrapbook of cuttings of the type of designs that held particular appeal for him. After the company he worked for was sold, the opportunity arose to turn those dreams into reality. Then, by chance, he met architect Robert Dye outside a friend's studio and, when they got talking, the rapport was instant. If proof that they were on the same wavelength were needed, the business card Dye gave him featured one of the designs that Powell had already cut out and collected.

The next stage was to find a site. Powell, who had looked at hundreds of sites and houses, finally found a 1950s house that was still lived in by the widow of the man who had built it. The area, principally residential, features Georgian and Edwardian terraces, along with newer buildings built on bomb-damaged sites, the result of wartime attacks on a nearby railway line. The 1950s house was actually the third built on the site, the previous two dating from 1820 and 1900. It was a great advantage to have an architect on board from the beginning, as Dye was able to visit the site before Powell bought it and advise him on its potential.

Equally sympathetic was the reaction of the local planners. Unlike many London authorities, the borough of Southwark has a reputation for encouraging modern architecture, and is averse to pastiche. Aside from the usual height and density restrictions, and a few minor details, the scheme was received very positively.

The initial plan was to remodel the property, keeping its shell and adding an extension at the rear. Once work began, however, it was clear that the house was in a very poor structural state; the more they tried to save it, the more of it fell down. Now all that remains of the original house is part of one internal wall. The central structural wall was built of bricks recovered from the site, remnants of all three previous properties. Otherwise the structure is timber-frame over a 190cm (6ft) concrete slab.

Powell, who was the build's project manager, had been extremely fortunate in his choice of architect. It was a different matter when it came to the first contractor he hired. After suffering weeks of delay, excuses and intimidation, Powell managed to find another team to take over the build, a group of Australians who had had ten years' experience building timber-frame houses. They varied the original plans and built to a stronger code.

ABOVE: The sleek modern design of this detached urban house was positively welcomed by local planners. The previous house on the site had been built in the 1950s and was in very poor condition. The basic structure is timber over a concrete slab.

From that point, until the build was finished two years after the initial start date, work proceeded very smoothly. The only nail-biting moment came with the installation of the 2.74m x 2.44m (9ft x 8ft) double-glazed unit that projects from the second floor. As the house is on a bus route, the use of a crane was not permitted. Instead, the builders took out the staircase, stood on stepladders and heaved the entire 450kg (1,000lb) unit up into the second floor while Powell sat outside in his car for a nervous five minutes trying not to look.

The three-storey house – some 230sq m (2,500sq ft) – now provides a home for Powell, his partner, award-winning comedian Jenny Eclair, and their daughter. On the ground floor, the main living accommodation is arranged in a simple circulation path with a front hall leading to a 'winter room', then to a 'summer room' on the same level facing the garden. A dining area takes up the rear and leads to a long, thin kitchen at the front. Upstairs is the master bedroom, dressing room and bathroom, along with

a study, guest room and wet room. On the third level is their daughter's bedroom and bathroom.

Materials are bold and striking. The roof is covered with the palest of felts, so that it almost disappears against the sky. Externally, upper walls are clad in Russian redwood stained black, while lower walls are rendered in a finish that contains flecks of mica. The same render is used on internal walls. All skirtings (baseboards) are shadow-gapped, the galvanized-steel edging lending a crispness of definition, while doors run floor to ceiling. On the ground level Powell wanted a poured rubber floor, but was aware installation can be difficult. Instead, he sourced a German rubber tile that comes in metre-square sizes. The stairs are made of oak; elsewhere, the flooring is birch ply in 1.2m (4ft) squares, washed white and treated with three coats of matt seal.

Simple but beautifully detailed, the house has a serene and tranquil mood. The projecting window boxes, which are such a feature of the elevation, have glazed tops and sides that provide beguiling slivers of views.

ABOVE: The main living areas downstairs are arranged in a simple circulation path. In the 'winter room' there is a contemporary wood-burning fireplace and log store.

LEFT: A view of the dining area, with its narrow horizontal window overlooking the passageway to the side of the house. All skirtings (baseboards) are shadow-gapped, an elegant detail that lends crispness to the finishes.

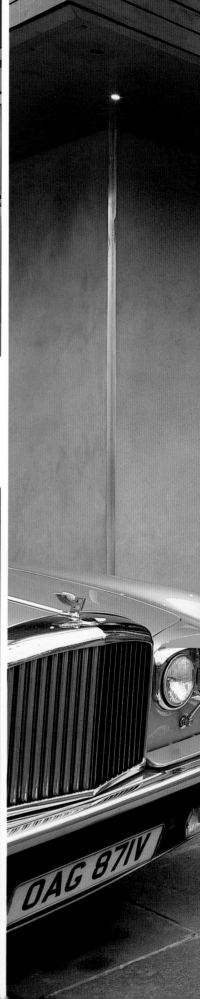

ABOVE: A relatively narrow kitchen leads off the dining area. Powell sourced German rubber tiles, which come in large squares, for the flooring on the ground level.

RIGHT: Externally, the building is partially clad with Russian redwood stained black, with the rest of the walls finished in a render that contains flecks of mica.

BELOW: The sleek and uncluttered master bathroom is a serene, contemplative space.

RURAL

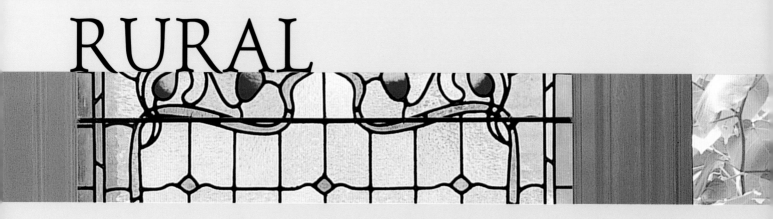

RETREATS

8

ARCHITECT: bloc design

Twenty minutes' drive west of Brisbane is this rainforest retreat, sited between a winding country road and a steep overgrown hillside with a creek running along its foot. Daryl O'Brien, a builder, who is also a keen gardener and cook, envisioned a house that would enable its owners to live as self-sufficiently and simply as possible. The secluded pavilion, which sits lightly on the land, is the result of a collaboration between O'Brien and his friend and now business partner, architect Peter Nelson. The scheme – which is O'Brien's own home and which he himself constructed – took a few years to realize; at the end of it the two went into partnership together.

58

Nelson produced the first sketches for the house while he was still in the final year of his architecture degree. From that point, the ideas continued to evolve in numerous discussions about how O'Brien wanted to live. The single-storey pavilion is essentially three rooms: bedroom, bathroom and living/kitchen space. Although it occupies only 55sq m (592sq ft), it provides a richness of spatial experience that belies its modest scale.

Nelson's work has been informed by the attempt to reconcile two different approaches to building: the building as an object sited in a natural landscape, and the building as the means by which our experience of landscape is heightened and mediated. To that end, he has been influenced by his travels through Japan and trips to the United States, where he visited many Frank Lloyd Wright buildings. Closer to home, the work of Brit Andresen and Peter O'Gorman has been another inspiration.

In this instance Nelson has responded to the landscape by conceiving the design around two alternative routes, so that the house unfolds as you walk through it or around it, and the whole is never revealed at once. 'Clip-on' boxes, which house the bathroom and daybed, further integrate the building with its setting while meeting basic functional requirements. From the exterior, the house appears to float over the site. The ground drops away to the creek, and the building almost seems to have been inserted between the trees. The pitch of the roof is inclined towards the hill.

The two entry/exit points on opposite sides of the pavilion set up the alternative routes, addressing two very different landscapes, one wild and one domesticated. The southern, or formal, entry is the culmination of a rainforest walk running parallel to the creek. Timber decks rise up to a solid door set in a wall clad in plywood stained black. From there one is

ABOVE LEFT: The less formal side of the pavilion has views over a vegetable garden. Walls are clad with compressed fibre cement panels painted white.

ABOVE: The sleeping area is minimally screened from the main living space by reclaimed elevator doors.

59

ushered into the main living space, dominated by a breathtaking view of the hillside and creek through the 4m (13ft) glazed end wall. A window box overlooking a vegetable garden provides a cosy seating area opposite the fireplace. Past the kitchen area, built in along one wall, a sliding panel connects to a bedroom, while a bathroom in another protruding box fitted with a roller door forms a 'gangway' between the sleeping area and the bush. The less formal entry, on the northern side, leads from the driveway along a narrow walkway past the vegetable garden and into the kitchen via corner doors. On this side of the house, windows are smaller in scale, framing the views of the elevated vegetable plot.

The building is timber-frame, and its roof structure is a sandwich of hardwood rafters, ceiling ply, battens, insulation and galvanized sheeting. Flat metal sheeting is used as an oversized flashing. These separate elements are peeled back and layered to feather the edge of the roof. On the end wall, the rafters turn down to become the vertical mullions of the large glass window, and visually relate to the tree trunks of the surrounding rainforest.

The main floor frame incorporates a hardwood ply skin over in-line beams and joists;

the window box is a raised timber seat with sliding glass panels. Rainforest timbers were used sparingly throughout. On exterior walls, compressed fibre cement sheeting painted white on the 'domestic' side of the house contrasts with ply sheeting stained black on the side facing the rainforest. Internally, there is a similar contrast between white-painted plasterboard and warm ply cladding. Sydney blue gum was used for the kitchen cabinets and benchtops. A reclaimed stained-glass window forms a glowing accent of light and colour in the bedroom's end wall. External hardwood decking is treated with a natural oil finish. Landscaping materials include hardwood sleepers, stone and timber walling and river pebbles.

The pavilion, no less than the care evident in its siting, displays a deep respect for nature. In section, the staggering of the building on the floor grid provides landscape views from every room; the façade seems to undulate between the trees. Down by the creek, O'Brien has begun an extensive programme of replanting, while the elevated vegetable garden supplies fresh food for the table. Here, simplicity is not lowest common denominator functionalism, but a considered and contemplative distillation of the essential activities of everyday life.

ABOVE LEFT: The less formal side of the pavilion has views over a vegetable garden. Walls are clad with compressed fibre cement panels painted white.
ABOVE: The sleeping area is minimally screened from the main living space by reclaimed elevator doors.

61

LEFT: A dramatic glazed end wall, extending up to 4m (13ft) provides breathtaking views of the surrounding rainforest. The house has been so sensitively sited it appears to have almost been inserted amongst the trees.

RIGHT: The bathroom is located in another projecting box. Cabinetry and flooring are made of Sydney blue gum and there is a fixed glass shower screen. Entrance to the bathroom is via a roller door.

9

green oak lodge, WEST CHILLA, DEVON, UK

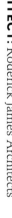

ARCHITECT: Roderick James Architects

Inspiration for dream houses can come from almost anywhere. For some people, it may come from a project that they have seen featured in a magazine; for others, it may be a house that they have visited that sparks the imagination. Some would-be self-builders are particularly drawn to the work of an individual architect. A brief five-minute segment on a popular television home makeover programme was all that it took to convince the Elstons that they had found their ideal home. The feature they had seen showed a couple who had built an oak-frame barn house, and from that moment the Elstons were determined to do the same.

64

The Elstons, who were nearing retirement, had lived in older houses all of their lives and particularly liked the traditional local building style, the Devon long house. What they knew from experience, however, was that old houses tend to be dark. A new barn house promised to be the best of both worlds, offering period charm, but with modern advantages, plenty of light and low upkeep and maintenance. They contacted the suppliers of the oak frame mentioned on the television programme and began planning their new house.

The first step was to find a site. They were determined to stay in the area and, rather than look further afield, kept in constant contact with local agents. A year of searching later and they finally found what they were looking for: a beautiful plot a third of a mile down an unmade lane overlooking Dartmoor and on the fringes of Forestry Commission land. As soon as they saw it, they offered the asking price.

The site, though ideal, came with certain conditions attached. It had already received outline planning permission for a bungalow, the foundations of which had already been laid. These foundations were in a different part of the plot to where the Elstons wanted to build their house. Also on the site was a modern barn, and a condition of the permission was that it should be used for some form of rural business. This is a type of condition which is quite common in areas of the UK where there are declining levels of employment, and is designed to keep job opportunities open for local people.

The Elstons made their offer on condition of obtaining permission for their own plans, which entailed moving the position of the proposed building to the top of the hill and building a barn house rather than a bungalow. After another year, permission was finally granted and work could get under way.

ABOVE: After a year of searching, the Elstons found their perfect site, overlooking Dartmoor. The structure is a traditional green oak-frame barn house, with windows all down the south-facing side. 'Cruck' construction uses naturally grown curved timber members.

65

LEFT: The main
bedroom is located
on the first floor
beyond the living
area. A pair of French
doors, one of five
on the south-facing
elevation, provides
access to the outdoors
as well as plenty of
natural light.

The scheme the Elstons submitted to the planners had been drawn up by Wray McCann, an architect working for Roderick James, who had pioneered the development of the barn house. The Elstons visited a number of other examples of this type of dwelling and discussed the type of accommodation that they required and could afford, as well other features, such as dormer windows and galleries, that they especially liked. The result was a long, one-and-a-half-storey oak-frame house with glazing all along the southern side.

Now retired, the Elstons sold their former home to finance the build, and moved into a caravan on site where they could oversee the work. The green oak frame, delivered on a truck, went up in just two and a half days. The traditional 'cruck' structure uses naturally grown curved members.

After the frame was in place, the next stage of the works was undertaken by two builders who were friends of the couple. With the house completed 18 months later, the entire

ABOVE: Detail of the kitchen area, slotted in underneath the larger of the two galleries. Many of the internal surfaces and finishes are wooden. Doors and storage cupboards are a mixture of oak and painted pine, and were made by the couple's son.

RIGHT: The cruck structure is boldly expressed on the interior of the house. The main living area is a generous space open to the rafters, extending from the kitchen through to a dining area, with a sitting area positioned around a wood-burning stove.

building process not only went very smoothly, but was enjoyable as well – a definite plus.

With two galleries at either end of the house, the layout of internal accommodation is very straightforward. Inside the front door there is a shower and utility room to the right; a guest bedroom also leads off the hall. A staircase gives access to the larger of the two galleries, which is open to the rafters and has a window in the gable end. This is used as a home office and seating area. Downstairs, the main living area is one generous space, with a kitchen installed under the gallery leading to a dining area, then to a sitting area open right up to the eaves and arranged around a cosy wood-burning stove which supplements the underfloor heating. Beyond the living area is the main bedroom and bathroom. From the master bedroom, another staircase connects to the second gallery. This has a balcony leading off it and is used as a storage area.

The Elstons love the look of wood. Not only are the timber members of the frame exposed, but many of the surfaces and finishes are wooden, too. The flooring is new pine painted with floor paint; doors and storage cupboards are a mixture of oak and painted pine. Internal walls are also panelled in wood and painted. The external wood walls are tanalized, while the roof is made of slate.

For the Elstons, one of the house's greatest assets is the quality of light. Two dormer windows light the larger of the two galleries, and rooflights over the living area bring bright top lighting down into the space. Ranged along the south-facing elevation are five pairs of French doors, the central one of which is aligned with French doors on the north side of the house. On summer days, with the doors wide open and the ground falling away to a view over Dartmoor, the house is more than ever the perfect marriage of old and new.

FAR LEFT: A simple open timber staircase provides access to an upper gallery.
ABOVE LEFT: Much of the interior finishes are wooden. The bathroom is clad in painted tongue-and-groove panelling.
ABOVE: The larger of the two galleries at either end of the house is used as a home office and extra seating area.

10

mill lawn cottage, NEW FOREST, HAMPSHIRE, UK

ARCHITECT: John Pardey Architects

A chronic shortage of space, particularly outdoor space, was what prompted one couple to leave the city for the countryside. With three growing children to be considered, their previous home and its tiny garden was beginning to feel cramped, and none of the properties they could afford in the vicinity gave the couple what they were looking for. As if exchanging south London for Hampshire was not already a big enough step, they set themselves another challenge by deciding to build their own home. The site they acquired, 0.7 hectares (1.7 acres) of idyllic countryside in the New Forest, took up about half their allotted budget.

The project, however, was no leap in the dark. Both husband and wife are engineers, and the husband's father is an architect, which meant that they already had a working familiarity with spatial design and structure. To refine their ideas and gain a broad sense of what was possible, they took advantage of London's annual 'Open House' weekend, when the public can visit private architect-designed houses all over the capital. The result of their viewings and deliberations was a detailed three-page brief which set out their specifications and wishes in full. Central to the brief was their desire to have a house that was 'extremely modern with a high attention to detail'.

The architect the couple chose to fulfil this brief was John Pardey, whose practice is based in a town near the land they had purchased. Pardey, who had built a modern house for himself, had long cherished the ambition to build a contemporary courtyard

house; right from the project's beginning, the match between clients and professional was a sympathetic one.

Existing planning constraints had already limited the amount of floor area that could be built on the site. Also, while the couple wanted a modern house, they were still keen that it should blend with its setting rather than impose or intrude upon it. In keeping with the verdant surroundings of Hampshire's New Forest, the resulting design was no brash urban upstart, but modest, calm and simple. Unfortunately, that was not the way the local parish council was to see it. When the designs for the house went into planning, objections were raised on the grounds that the house was out of keeping with its context. It might well have been a case of back to the drawing board were it not for a local planning officer who overruled the objections and allowed the scheme to proceed.

ABOVE: Situated in idyllic countryside in the New Forest, this contemporary house is L-shaped in plan, with a single storey 'stable block' providing accommodation for the family's children.

ABOVE: The house under construction. The lower level is blockwork construction; the first floor structure is timber. The structural difference is echoed on the façade.

RIGHT: Large expanses of glass bathe the interior in natural light and provide beguiling views of the stunning setting.

The couple had specified that they would prefer a building that did not read as a single mass, but rather as a collection of linked shapes. With the two-storey barn-like structure connected to a single-storey wing reminiscent of a stable block, the building is L-shaped in plan, forming a partially enclosed courtyard at the rear. The ground level is of blockwork construction, while the upper storey is timber, a difference expressed on the façades, where the lower rendered storey gives way to western red cedar cladding above. The pitched roof is clad in black zinc.

The internal planning provides a broadly open layout of distinct areas serving different functions – the couple did not feel that loft-style spaces were appropriate for the setting. The dwelling's main entrance, down a garden path that runs through a wildflower meadow, is sited where the single-storey wing meets the main house and opens into a dramatic

hall/dining area. The L-shaped kitchen looks out over the front and wraps around the corner under the main staircase. Internal openings provide slices of view through to the sitting room with its central focus, an open fire on a concrete hearth. On the level above are the master bedroom and a wet room.

The single-storey wing provides a more or less linear arrangement running the long side of the L. Immediately to the left of the main entrance is a study, followed by a guest toilet, and a guest room and en suite bathroom. Three further bedrooms and a large bathroom are for the children. These rooms have windows that open like traditional stable doors, onto an outside terrace.

Throughout, attention to detail is evident in the high quality of finishes and materials. Many of the elements are bespoke. Aside from the limestone in the hall and the rubber flooring used in all the bathrooms, the flooring

BELOW: Throughout, the house is beautifully detailed and finished. A recessed horizontal strip window frames a view in a bathroom, which is neatly clad in large mosaic tiles. While white oiled oak is largely used throughout the rest of the house, flooring in the bathroom is rubber, a more practical choice.

RIGHT: The kitchen, which is L-shaped, looks out over the front of the house and wraps under the main staircase. The counter is made of basalt, with generous base units underneath. Although the house is not fully open-plan, internal windows and openings serve to keep it light and airy.

FAR LEFT: A glazed gable end, augmented by a narrow recessed vertical window, fills the master bedroom with light. Storage is built-in.

LEFT: The L-shaped plan of the house and wing create a private courtyard at the rear.

BELOW: On the courtyard side of the house, three large sliding windows connect directly with an outdoor deck. The timber decking provides a seamless transition. The main stairs are made of folded steel.

is white oiled oak. The kitchen counter is basalt, and generous storage is provided in the base units underneath. The staircase is made of folded steel. The basic palette of materials, both indoor and out is natural and neutral in tone, in keeping with the country setting. However, this reticence is enlivened by vivid splashes of colour that occur throughout the house, striking a particularly uplifting note in the children's bedrooms. In the bedrooms and bathrooms, built-in furniture and storage makes the most of the available area.

A particularly ingenious feature is the wine cellar concealed under a hatch in the study floor – open it up and a spiral staircase descends 2m (6½ft) below giving access to wall-mounted racks.

As beautifully designed and detailed as the house is, there is no doubt where the true focus of attention lies. Every opportunity is taken to merge indoors with out, and fantastic views are not distant prospects, but an integral part of the design itself. Three huge sliding windows connect the living areas with an outdoor deck, while a glazed gable end in the master bedroom bathes the upper storey in light. Unlike traditional cottages, which are often inward-looking and dark, this modern country house embraces its setting with open and enthusiastic arms.

richard priest house, KARE KARE, AUCKLAND, NEW ZEALAND

ARCHITECT: Hillery Priest Architecture Ltd

The tiny hamlet of Kare Kare (population of permanent residents, 350) is located 45 minutes' drive west of the city of Auckland. A popular local resort in summer – 60 per cent of the houses are holiday homes – Kare Kare is situated in a remote and rugged part of New Zealand's west coast, miles from the nearest store. And if the dramatic scenery looks familiar, that is because the beach was the haunting backdrop to the film *The Piano*. Perched high on a cliff overlooking the settlement of Kare Kare is the family home of Richard Priest and his wife, Sue Curtling. The site was originally part of a farm, an 'island' within Auckland's largest national park, the Waitakere Ranges.

When the farm was no longer economically viable, the owner divided the land into 4-hectare (10-acre) lots and sold them off – which is where Richard Priest and Sue Curtling came in.

The couple had previously spent a lot of time on the beach and in the hills, and knew that they wanted to live on the west coast. There were other considerations on their wish list. Sue wanted grazing land for horses, and they both wanted water on the site or running through it, so they could use it. They found the property one day when they were on their way to look at another site. At that time it had an old house on it, with a hedge completely obscuring the stunning view. Once the couple had seen what was beyond the hedge, and walked over the land to find a large dam and a number of open areas that could be converted to pasture, their minds were made up. They made an offer on the spot, leaving Richard's watch behind as a gesture of good faith until the

real-estate agent returned from an open house she was running that day to conclude the deal.

The original house was too small to accommodate the family. Its replacement, designed by Richard, took shape over time. At the outset, they had no formal brief but to house themselves and keep out the weather. As the design evolved, however, it took its cues from the surrounding landscape. The basic concept is of a cross sitting within a circle, with the cross, like a compass, pointing west–east and north–south. This form made it possible to create different external areas sheltered from the wind, sun or rain. The back courtyard, for example, which is rarely used in winter, is a favourite summer spot, being cool, green and close to the water. The house is oriented to the northwest, which means that it picks up warmth from the sun during the day. Only in the darkest winter months is it necessary to turn on the heating.

ABOVE LEFT: Few sites are more dramatic than this hilltop location in New Zealand, over-looking the beach that was used as a location in the film *The Piano*. The site was part of a farm that was subdivided and sold off.

ABOVE: The beautiful and rugged west coast continues north from Kare Kare, where the house is located, to the equally spectacular Piha beach.

81

RIGHT: The house is securely anchored into the hillside.
BELOW: The kitchen is minimally separated from the living area by an island bench with a terrazzo top.

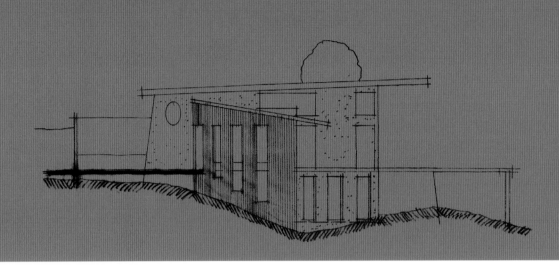

RIGHT: Furnishings are an eclectic mix of Scandinavian modern and salvaged and retro finds, along with inherited pieces. The fireplace is plastered concrete fireblock.

Arranged over two levels, the house has four bedrooms – two for the children, a main bedroom and a guest room. The principal living areas are interconnected, with the kitchen minimally divided from the rest of the living area by an island bench and the change of activity further signalled by the flooring – polished concrete with underfloor heating to the rear, giving way to pine floorboards in the rest of the house. There are also two bathrooms, a small study, a large walk-in storeroom, a walk-in wardrobe, a laundry room housed in a cupboard and an outside bathtub, where you can soak by starlight and listen to the ocean.

The house is a rendered timber-frame structure with a Zincalume butterfly roof and aluminium-frame windows. It took about a year to construct, from the first cut into the soil until the day they moved in. Sue and Richard were in no particular hurry, and it's a laid-back part of the world. Internally, materials are simple – plastered concrete fireblock for the fireplace, terrazzo for the benchtops and cedar

cladding in the dining area. In the kitchen is a commercial glass-fronted beer fridge picked up when a local café closed. Furnishings are a similarly eclectic mixture of inherited pieces, salvage and Danish modern. The bedroom sideboard and sofa are Richard's designs, while the work of local artists and craftspeople is on prominent display. The decorative palette echoes the soft colours of the bush and sea.

With expanses of glass at the front taking in the sweeping views, and the precipitous perch on the cliff edge, the effect might have been a little alarming were it not for the fact that the house is securely dug into the hillside at the rear. Approached from the curved front, a series of square windows lead the eye into the interior. A window cut into a concrete wall beside a reflecting pool frames and mediates the vast panorama. The balance of openness and security makes it a peaceful haven, a sanctuary literally poised on the edge of the world.

ABOVE: A window cut into an external concrete wall mediates between the house and its setting, framing the views. The garden features native trees and plants.

LEFT: The master bedroom on the first floor has a large window providing panoramic views of the sea. The curtains are made of peacock blue satin and the cabinet was designed by Richard Priest.

FAR LEFT: The couple built an outdoor tub so they could soak under the stars while listening to the ocean.

contemporary cabin, NEAR BILBAO, SPAIN

ARCHITECT: AV62 Arquitectos

As everyone knows, finding a suitable site can be a considerable challenge for those setting out to build their own home. When that elusive piece of land finally presents itself, it can be tempting to snap it up before carrying out investigations as to its development potential. In Spain's Basque country, 20km kilometres (12.4 miles) from Bilbao, this contemporary family house is situated high up a wooded hillside on the fringes of an old fishing village. The dramatic site, which had been acquired by the clients before they commissioned the design, offered a unique opportunity to connect with nature. The extreme slope, however, posed a number of technical problems.

Architects often find themselves placed in the position of having to deal with the challenges thrown up by unusual sites. A site may be awkwardly shaped; there may be existing trees that have to be designed around; in urban areas, there are numerous sensitive issues to do with adjoining properties and overlooking. Here, however, the problems were twofold: the severe incline and the poor ground conditions. When Toño Foraster was first shown the site where his clients intended to build, his initial reaction, understandably, was a rather dubious 'Where?' Although the site comprised some 2,000sq m (21,500sq ft), most of it was unusable. Foraster's solution, which was to create a long single-storey house that seems almost to hover over the edge of the valley, provides exactly the type of connection to nature that the clients wanted. In the original scheme, there was no garden at all, which served to emphasize this 'floating' quality. Now, however,

a vertical green wall, which takes vegetation up the slope, shades a small outdoor terrace.

Unsurprisingly, the most difficult part of the build proved to be the foundations. The site is located in a northern part of Spain which receives a high degree of rainfall in winter; coupled with its slope, this meant that the soil was poor and the ground conditions were far from stable. Excavations had to go down a long way before rock was encountered. The foundation itself was a thick concrete slab, much thicker than normal, and the process of constructing it was prolonged due to the fact that there was no direct access to the site. Both materials and equipment had to be brought down from the road some 12m (40ft) above where the house is now located.

After the foundations were in place, the rest of the build proceeded very smoothly and quickly. Foraster had chosen a structural system which could be assembled like a kit of

ABOVE: Despite the considerable technical challenges posed by the site, this contemporary cabin on a wooded hillside makes the most of a stunning location. Windows all along the south-facing wall provide views of a river and fishing village. AV62 Architectos is a partnership of Toño Foraster and Victoria Garriga.

87

ABOVE: The timber-frame house under construction. The most difficult part of the build was laying the foundations.

RIGHT: The house appears to hover over its site. The gable end, where the master bedroom is located, is part glazed, part clad in cedar. The roof covering is made of zinc.

parts. The timber frame, comprising laminated pine trusses, was specially commissioned and made, an adaptation of a factory-built system. On the house's north wall, solid timber panels, 15cm (6in) in section, were slotted between the columns; most of the remaining walls were glazed, with one gable end part clad in cedar. Because this form of construction is dry – unlike concrete or masonry – it is very quick to go up. The roof covering is zinc.

The house is the main home of a couple with young children and provides most of the accommodation on one floor. From the floor to the top of the roof measures 6m (19ft 8in), and the main living areas are high, clear spaces. Bed and bath platforms are tucked into the generous ceiling void at the more enclosed end of the house. To keep the space as free and open as possible, the servicing and plant for heating and air conditioning are located underneath the house.

A decked terrace leads into the main living area with its open fireplace housed in a free-standing white cube. A half-height plastered divider, providing shelving for books and a place for the television, serves as a minimal partition between this area and the kitchen/dining area. A smaller, covered terrace is immediately adjacent to the dining room, so that the family can eat outdoors even if it is raining. Beyond the kitchen/dining area are three bedrooms. Two of these, for the children, are arranged with bathrooms on the ground level and platforms above for study or sleeping. In the main bedroom, it is the bathroom that is on the upper level.

The orientation of the house is towards the south, with views towards a distant river. Through the use of large expanses of glazing, the open and airy design makes the most of the commanding, elevated position in the hills. The gable end where the living room is

located is entirely glazed, and so is the south-facing wall. On the north wall, bands of horizontal window provide additional natural light. The windows are double-glazed and laminated, for reasons of security as well as indoor climate control. The clients have reported that the house requires little supplementary heating or cooling – when it is warm, opening the windows is enough to generate cooling through breezes inside the house.

When it comes to decoration, the choices have deliberately been kept as simple and restrained as possible so as not to detract from the expansive views. Inside, the trusses are exposed and the sloping planes of the ceiling are painted white. The flooring is white pine. Floor-level lights sunk into the exterior decking provide atmospheric effects. Indoors, uplighters concealed in the structure bathe the incline of the roof and accentuate the soaring volume of the space.

ABOVE LEFT: The windows are double-glazed and laminated to aid internal climate control and as a security measure.

ABOVE RIGHT: The panoramic view from the master bedroom.

RIGHT: The main living area extends to an outdoor deck with recessed floor lights. Uplighters indoors are concealed in the structure.

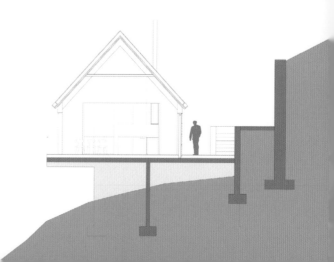

super e house, DEVIOCK, CORNWALL, UK

ARCHITECT: Catchfrench Design

After five years of looking, Sarah and Douglas Stewart were about to abandon their search for a site in Cornwall when one bitter, misty January day, they stumbled onto this beautiful plot overlooking the sea. Almost immediately, they knew it was what they had been looking for. Overgrown with brambles, and with a derelict bungalow in situ, it was far from what most people might consider a rustic idyll. It was not until Douglas clambered onto the bungalow roof on a visit two weeks later that they even realized there were sea views in two directions. Their first offer was rejected; fortunately, their second, which took them to their budget's limit, was accepted.

Sarah had dreamed of building her own home since her teens. And, given his successful career in the construction industry, it is not surprising, perhaps, that Douglas should have felt the same way. The house they have built reflects the fact that over the years both have grown more and more convinced of the need to build sustainably.

After the land purchase, they contacted local architects Catchfrench Design, who specialize in sustainable building. Together with John Wilkes, a member of the practice, the Stewarts developed the design for a two-storey house to take advantage of the views. Although this was a storey higher than the existing bungalow, the proposed scheme placed the new house further down the site, at a level where the second-storey roofline would be no higher than the old bungalow roof. The environmental features of the design pleased the planners, and the process of obtaining permission went smoothly.

The first bespoke Super E design in Britain, the house is a prefabricated timber-frame structure that was made in Canada. In the past, prefab has often been synonymous in people's minds with shoddy, substandard and bland. Nowadays, this is certainly not the case. Like many prefab systems, the Super E is available as standard kits of various sizes, but also allows for individual specification, provided that at least 60 per cent of the total product is ordered. In the Stewarts' case, that meant the house kit came complete with doors, skirtings (baseboards), architraves and windows; they decided to source the kitchen and some of the other interior materials themselves.

Most crucially, the environmental credentials of the Super E house could not be higher. Super E houses are designed to be airtight and are highly insulated, which means that they are incredibly energy-efficient and low in carbon emissions. Every Super E house has to pass a

ABOVE: This two-storey house was built to individual specification using the Super E prefabricated system, an environmentally friendly system manufactured in Canada. Super E houses are designed to be airtight. The system can be applied to any style of house. Super E certification can only be achieved using a registered Super E builder.

93

ABOVE: The house occupies a plot of land overlooking the sea.

RIGHT: The master bedroom is filled with light from the gable window. All the skirtings (baseboards), doors, architraves and windows were included in the kit. The flooring is bamboo.

'blower door test' to ensure that windows and other openings are as tightly sealed as possible and there are no leaks. Most new houses have 10 air changes an hour – air lost through gaps in window and door frames, and so on – which represents a direct energy loss. Super E houses achieve a mere 1.5 air changes an hour.

Insulation levels are very high. There is a 300mm (11¾in) layer of cellulose insulation in the cathedral ceiling and 150mm (5¹¹⁄₁₂in) in the internal walls. The exterior is insulated with 38mm (1½in) of sheet insulation. The result is that the house requires a fraction of the heating that other new homes require.

In the plant room, there is a heat recovery ventilation unit and a heat pump which takes energy from the ground and converts it into electricity for the underfloor heating and the hot-water cylinders. Only a small boost from the mains supply is required to bring the water up to a high enough temperature for showering.

Investment in the plant is high, but the payback is low running costs and low carbon emissions.

The choice of a timber-frame structure over masonry construction was also inspired by environmental concerns. 'Embodied energy', which is the sum of all the energy required to produce and transport a material, is much lower in the case of timber than it is for materials such as brick, block, concrete and plastic. By choosing timber, the Stewarts were opting for a sustainable, renewable resource that minimizes carbon dioxide emissions. The main timber used was cedar. The roof is slate, while the plinth at the base of the house is Cornish stone from nearby Lantoom Quarry.

Douglas spent one summer building the foundations and laying the services. Once the components arrived, shipped from Canada in three containers, the house took less than two months to construct. All the finishing materials were chosen to be as sustainable,

low-emission and energy-efficient as possible, and include bamboo for the flooring, walls made of compressed gypsum and recycled paper, and water-based nontoxic paints. The only compromise were the MDF cabinet doors in the kitchen, which they plan to replace at a later date. Recently, Douglas completed a course in sewage disposal and has been constructing a reed bed in the garden for water treatment.

The house, on two floors, has four bedrooms, with the ground floor given over to spare rooms and an additional kitchen which their grown-up children and their families use when they stay. On the level above, natural light pours in through a glass gable and cathedral window facing the sea. The changing light and panoramic views forge a real connection with the spectacular setting. The airtight house has an exceptionally relaxing ambience – and is warm enough on even the chilliest days to wander around in bare feet, a feel-good factor of the first order.

ABOVE LEFT: The house is arranged over two stories, with guest accommodation on the ground floor and the main living areas and master bedroom on the level above.

ABOVE: The kitchen was sourced by the clients. The house is so warm and well insulated that it is possible to wander around in bare feet even on chilly days.

FAR LEFT: The timber-frame house is clad in cedar. Douglas now offers consultancy within the eco self-build market.

dirk pien house, BERGEN, THE NETHERLANDS

ARCHITECT: Soeters Van Eldonk Ponec Architecten

With its tiered, sheltering thatched roof, this villa is located some 50km (30 miles) from Amsterdam on the fringes of a small community that has attracted many artists over the years. Many older local houses were built in the style of the Amsterdam School and are shaped like ships; other vernacular buildings feature thatching or timber cladding. The design Sjoerd Soeters came up with for the couple who owned the site reflects both the woodland setting behind a dune landscape and the local building styles. The ship-like form of the two structures, one an L-shaped house and the other a garage, is further exaggerated by the low rise of land at the front of the site.

The design took longer to gestate than to build. The brief was simple: two bedrooms, a master bedroom and a guest room, an office for the husband and a studio for the wife. The wife, an enthusiastic and accomplished cook, wanted the kitchen to be large and the focus of the main living areas. Long, amicable planning sessions followed, with clients and architect discussing every detail of the design.

Equally protracted, but more frustrating, was the process of obtaining official permission for the scheme. The authorities wanted the house to occupy no more than half the width of the site and to be placed centrally, so that there was green on both sides; they also wanted the garage building tucked behind and hidden. Progress was halted for some four months until approval was finally won for both structures in their present positioning.

The clients specifically wanted a thatched roof. Soeters, who had never designed one

before, came up with a striking contemporary solution. Normally thatching is topped out by round roof tiles set in concrete, which can look clumsy. In this case, copper sheet is used both on the roofline and to separate the three horizontal layers. The metal strips have a cleaner look, while the copper oxide destroys any green growth in the thatch. The roof is not pierced with any openings, but forms a strong connecting element for both structures, which are pulled apart to frame a view of a mature tree. Hunkered down, like an overturned hull, from the front the house is hidden and protected by the low roofline; while the garden elevation is more open and airy.

The house's basic structure is comprised of load-bearing brick walls with a steel skeleton to support the roof and create the large vaulted spans. The thatch was bound over a plywood understructure. In plan, the house is L-shaped, with the kitchen, located at the hinge of the L,

ABOVE: Two views of the villa. From the front elevation, the house and garage resemble an overturned hull pulled apart to form two structures. From the rear, the house has a much more open aspect, with large expanses of glazing. The two buildings frame a view of a tree.

99

ABOVE: The house under construction. The thatched roof is supported by a steel skeleton resting on load-bearing brick walls.

RIGHT: A small vestibule leads to the entrance hall. Double doors connect to the dining area and allow the entire space to be used for entertaining.

immediately accessible from the outside. A play of contrasting volumes creates a great sense of vitality. From the front entrance, a small low vestibule painted dark blue leads to a soaring vaulted space lit both ends by huge windows. A dining room leads off the hall and is located under the mezzanine. The kitchen connects the light, spacious living room with the dining room. The dark corridor leads from the hall to the living room. At the garden end, the roof is brought low near the brick-built chimney to create a more intimate corner. The main bathroom is located on the upper level at the plan's centre. It has no windows, except for a narrow opening where the lower portion of the roof moves into the upper. This indirect, high-level light gives a great sense of intimacy.

Materials used throughout are natural and in keeping with the Nordic aesthetic. The main flooring downstairs is a very pale limestone, laid diagonally. Flooring in the kitchen, vestibule

and bathroom is large tiles of greenish slate. On the stairs and mezzanine level, flooring is maple, while the bedroom carpet is undyed pure wool. Walls are painted pristine white; a blue tint gives the white extra freshness.

Lighting was a key concern. Wall washers and other discreetly hidden fittings give the house an entirely different feeling at night.

For Soeters, a particular delight of the project was that he was able to design all the fittings and fixtures himself, including the zigzag storage cupboards in the bathroom and special cabinets in the hall housing a collection of antique marriage boxes. These are made of maple and feature integral lighting. Mirror strips at the bases mean the cupboards appear to hover over the floor. In a delightful personal touch the front door handle is fashioned from a small tree branch brought back from a trek by dog sledge through Finland, a reminder of the natural elements the couple hold dear.

THIS PAGE: The bathroom has an intimate contemplative atmosphere, which is the result of high-level indirect lighting. Large tiles of greenish slate are used for flooring.

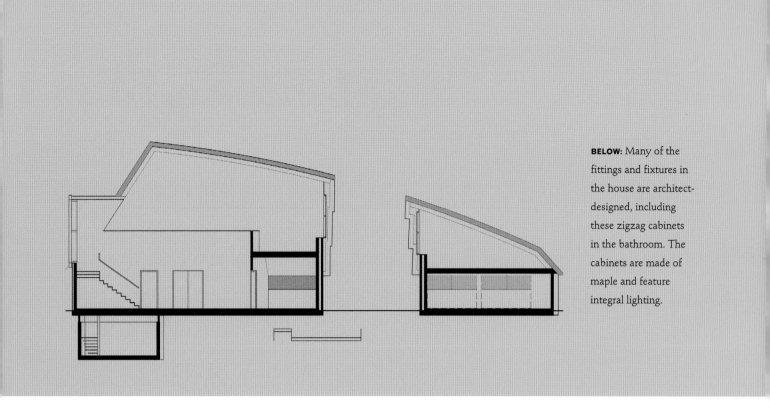

BELOW: Many of the fittings and fixtures in the house are architect-designed, including these zigzag cabinets in the bathroom. The cabinets are made of maple and feature integral lighting.

The thatched roof, which is not pierced with any openings, forms a strong connecting element for the structures of both house and garage, which are pulled apart to frame a view of a mature tree.

15

the old woodyard, HARGHAM, NORFOLK, UK

ARCHITECT: GreenYard Architecture

When the time came to retire and turn the running of the family estate over to their son, Sir Thomas and Lady Beevor decided to build a new house halfway down the drive from their ancestral seat. More radically, the house they chose to build was a modern eco-friendly lodge. On the face of it, nothing could be more different from Hargham Hall, the seventeenth-century manor house that has been owned and occupied by the Beevor family ever since its construction in 1690. Yet, in a sense, the thinking behind the new building demonstrates a similar attitude of trusteeship for future generations – in this case one founded on a desire to conserve the earth's rapidly diminishing resources.

Finding a site was easy. Neither husband nor wife wanted to leave the estate to which they were so devoted, and planning permission was obtained to build on the site of an old derelict woodyard in the grounds of the hall. From the outset, the Beevors were determined to build an eco-friendly house; when they visited the house of Neil Winder, a Norfolk architect specializing in eco-friendly design, they found an example of just what they were looking for. The result of their collaboration is a charming, traditional-style cottage that blends beautifully with its parkland setting.

The house has been specifically designed to cope with future changes in climate such as flooding or extremes of temperature. The elevation of the house some 90cm (3ft) over the ground protects against the possibility of flooding and also meant that only the ground underneath the supporting stilts needed to be disturbed, leaving behind as small a footprint

on the land as possible. Additionally, the foundations themselves were designed to minimize building settlement. Rainwater goods of a larger than standard section were used to promote quick run-off in heavy downpours. The use of 'breathing wall' construction means faster response to weather changes, and the south-facing roof pitches have an additional heat-reflective layer.

A central tenet of ecological design and building is to use local, sustainable materials wherever possible. In the case of this timber-frame, weatherboarded house, the materials employed could hardly be more local. In accordance with the Beevors' brief to the architect, more than 80 per cent of the wood used in building came from the woodlands on the estate where the house is sited, with the remainder originating from other local Norfolk estates. Furthermore, all of the timber, both softwoods and hardwoods, was processed in

ABOVE: This charming timber-clad house blends happily with its setting in the grounds of Hargham Hall. Much of the timber used in its construction came from the woodlands on the estate and were processed in the estate woodyard.

ABOVE: The process of construction was quick and simple. Three carpenters put up the frame using basic tools. The walls are highly insulated with recycled newspaper.

RIGHT: The vibrant palette of colours used internally was inspired by the work of the Swedish artist Karl Larsson. All paints are nontoxic.

the estate woodyard. Really, the name of the house could scarcely be more apposite.

The house is a timber-frame structure, built of softwoods such as Douglas fir, larch and some Corsican pine. The use of hardwoods, including ash, chestnut and cherry, which are slower growing and less sustainable for that reason, was reserved for floor finishes and thresholds only. Because of cutting restrictions at the estate woodyard and time pressures on the construction period, dimensions were kept to planks no more than 5.2m (17ft) in length. The external structure was quick and simple to build, and involved the services of only three carpenters working with basic tools – a traditional method of construction that would have been familiar 300 years ago when Hargham Hall itself was built. Further evidence of the eco-friendly spirit of this project can be found in the huge amounts of another wood-based product, newspaper,

which was used as insulation. The walls are air-permeable, which provides a fresh and healthy interior environment. Internally, timbers are left untreated.

Solar panels mounted on the roof generate energy for heating water. Internal planning is arranged to assist cross-flow ventilation, with key partitions in the kitchen, dining area, living room and hall stopped short of the ceiling to let air through, the same strategy also serving to lend a sense of generosity and enhance the connection with outdoors. Strategically placed 'spyholes' and hatches offer beguiling slices of view.

In planning and layout, the design also keeps an eye to the future. The master bedroom is situated downstairs along with the main living accommodation, which will prove increasingly practical as the couple grow older. The kitchen/dining/living area that forms the greater part of the ground floor level is

LEFT AND RIGHT: The house sits lightly on the land on supporting stilts.

BELOW: Surrounding planting includes wildflower lawns, a vegetable garden and reed beds which filter waste water. There is also a natural swimming pool.

BELOW RIGHT: Timber used in the construction of the house includes Douglas fir, larch and Corsican pine. Hardwoods such as ash, chestnut and cherry, were used for flooring and thresholds only. The layout was planned to aid cross-ventilation.

inclusive rather than entirely open-plan, and large south-facing windows bathe the interior in natural light.

While the house is traditional in style from the exterior, inside, brightly coloured surfaces strike a more contemporary note. The vibrant palette of colours that has been used in the indoor decoration was inspired by the work of the Swedish artist Karl Larsson. All of the paints used are nontoxic.

The house is designed and orientated to welcome nature with open arms, and it is surrounded by natural planting and wildflower lawns. But the setting also provides more practical benefits. All household waste is naturally treated, either through a composting system or through reed-bed filtration. There is even a large natural swimming pool, specially planted so that no chemicals need to be used to keep the water clear.

Proof of the success of the collaboration between architect and like-minded clients does not rest solely with the completion of the house. Sally Beevor project-managed the entire scheme. Since the Old Woodyard was completed she has worked in partnership with Neil Winder on several other GreenYard architectural projects.

PART

2

Before you get down to the practicalities of making your project happen, it's a good idea to acquaint yourself with all the options for self-build, even if you already have some notion of how you want to proceed. With further research and deliberation you might well find yourself considering a possibility that would never have occurred to you before, or perhaps you will find yourself changing your mind about which materials to use or structural system to adopt.

CREATIVE

REVIEW

Prefab used to have a dreary image, one that, in many people's minds, was synonymous with shoddy, temporary structures. Now, however, this entire sector has become much more sophisticated; some might say it is arguably the future of the building industry. More cost-effective than standard methods of building, prefabrication means factory-style efficiency can be brought to bear on the process of construction and dramatically shortens the time on site. In turn, that means there is much less chance for the build to be held up by bad weather – or lack of light, as in Scandinavian countries where this type of construction is very popular. For example, more than 90 per cent of Finnish homes are prefabricated. Prefab also addresses the real problem of skill shortages in certain sectors of the construction industry.

The ultimate prefab is the kit house. Many bespoke houses have prefabricated elements, more often than not the basic structural system. A kit house is entirely prefabricated, either as a basic weathertight shell to which interior surfaces and fittings are applied, or as a virtually complete home, right down to the last partition wall.

Like prefab, the kit house has an image problem. If you have been attracted to self-build because you want something out of the ordinary, you may think a kit house is not for you. Yet, while it is true that the majority of kit houses are traditional, even conservative, in design and appearance, a significant number of them are not, and this proportion is on the increase. Some kit houses can be customized to your specification; others are inherently more cutting edge. If you research the market, you might be pleasantly surprised to find a design that meets your needs and expectations. Alternatively, if

RIGHT: This elegant Australian pavilion could not be further from the stereotypical image of the prefab house. Sitting lightly on the land, this simple vacation house in New South Wales, with its sliding glass doors, recalls the refinement of Japanese architecture. The sheltered veranda is a contemporary version of a vernacular feature.

PREFABS AND KIT HOUSES

you are working with an architect to realize your project, he or she might be able to come up with a way of benefiting from the practical advantages of prefabricated elements within the context of an original design.

Kit houses remain the first choice for a significant proportion of self-builders for several good reasons. The first is that they remove a considerable degree of uncertainty from what can be a less than cut-and-dried process. If you buy a kit house from a reputable firm with a good track record in this type of manufacture, you know what you will get, you

know that your house will be structurally sound and you can be fairly confident that you will encounter no objections either from the planning or zoning department or from building inspectors, provided the design is compatible with local styles of building. Added to which, the time of the actual build will be cut dramatically. Some kits can go up in a matter of days. If you are not interested in making a bold architectural statement, but simply want a house that gives you the accommodation you want in the location of your choice, a kit house can be a good option.

As so much of the house is manufactured off site, companies specializing in kit houses (often known as 'package deal' companies) will request a significant amount of funds up front, so you need to have your cash flow in place. It's also fair to say that a kit house is not always the cheapest option for self-build; at the upper end of the market, kit houses most definitely fall into the luxury category. Across the sector, companies are in business to make a profit by making the build easier for you, but not necessarily cheaper. In other words, you get what you pay for. At the same time, while the actual build may be quick, you may have to wait for a significant period of time for the components to be manufactured and delivered, so the overall time required to complete your project might not be lessened significantly.

Most kit houses employ a timber-frame structure, although there are companies that produce brick and block houses (one company makes fully fitted concrete modules that can be assembled in 10 hours). Others specialize in steel-frame kits. Cladding is a different matter, and may vary from brick and stone to timber or metal and combinations of the same. Package-deal companies have expertise in local variations of style and can recommend materials and elevational details more likely to win favour with the authorities in a particular area. Even so, you are not obliged to stick within the boundaries of your regional vernacular. Many self-builders who opt for a kit house do so because they fancy the idea of a New England colonial house in the Surrey countryside, for example, and look abroad for companies that specialize in a particular building style. If this appeals, you may need to be prepared to make your aesthetic case to local planning authorities.

ABOVE: Kit houses can be just as durable as those built more conventionally. This house near the Hudson River, NY, erected in 1956, is an early example of a 'tech-built' house.

BELOW: The LV Kit Home is a prefab two-bedroom, two-bathroom vacation home designed by architect Rocio Romero. Units can be combined to make larger structures.

ABOVE: The Aperture House, designed by Vetter Denk Architects of Milwaukee, was conceived as an affordable private home using prefabricated elements. There are plans to bring the design to the mass market.

ABOVE RIGHT: New York-based architects LOT-EK specialize in using salvaged industrial components. This prefab structure is assembled out of shipping containers.

RIGHT: Prefabs and kit houses can be delivered whole or in parts direct to the site.

Most package-deal companies will allow you to make alterations to the stock plans and designs they offer so that your house meets all your specific requirements as closely as possible; there may be other changes they will recommend to smooth the planning process. Some companies offer a full design service which is not unlike that you would receive from an architect, the difference being that you cannot simply take the plans away and build the house yourself: signing up with a package-deal company commits you to the kit. In the same way, standard house designs as shown in company brochures are heavily protected by copyright law.

As is the case if you were working with an architect or other design professional, you need to be clear about the brief and your requirements from the outset. You stand a much better chance of getting what you want if you set up a healthy creative dialogue from the very beginning of a project.

Unusual prefabs

Prefabrication is nothing new. The American mail-order company Sears, Roebuck & Co produced home kits as early as 1908. In 1949 Charles and Ray Eames built the seminal Case Study House Number 8 entirely out of mass-produced components used in factory construction. Although the house was a one-off, it demonstrated that prefab does not have to mean traditional style or lowest common denominator in terms of quality.

Today, traditional design still dominates the prefab or kit market, but there are signs that this is beginning to change. Although not as widely available, there are some kit houses on the market that display more of a cutting-edge aesthetic and a number of architects across the world are currently producing modernist prototypes for reproduction using prefab techniques. One modular home that was recently launched is Glidehouse, designed by Michelle Kaufmann, which features sliding wood panels

that conceal storage and control light and ventilation. Such prefabricated modernist kits might soon bring affordable contemporary design to the housing sector, just as mass-market retailers such as IKEA have done for the modern interior. Geodesic domes, brainchild of the late American architect Buckminster Fuller, are also available in kit form.

Blurring the boundary between manufactured home and mobile home, architects such as Sean Godsell in Australia and LOT-EK, a New York-based practice, have experimented with the ultimate module, the shipping container. Godsell's Future Shack, a customization of a shipping container, was developed as a solution to the need for low-cost affordable housing. Abundant, cheap and structurally sound, shipping containers can be bolted into larger structures or combined in modular fashion, as exemplified by Quik House, a kit made from steel, shipping containers and cinder blocks, designed by Adam Kalkin.

Less quirky but still less conventional than mass-market designs are those kits which replicate vernacular building types such as the Scandinavian A-frame, the barn and the log cabin; one company even manufactures a 'Bali-style' kit house, constructed on an aluminium frame. With a decreasing supply of original barns to convert into homes, barn kits are a popular prefab option, particularly in the United States, where kit cabins and log houses are also sought after for second or holiday homes.

For the eco-minded, there are kit homes that embody environmentally friendly approaches. One large German manufacturer makes prefab houses that run on solar energy. Some Canadian and Scandinavian firms have airtight, highly energy-efficient prefabs that are low in carbon emissions; the Super E timber-frame system from Canada is a good example (see pages 92–7). Where a complete kit is not required, the use of prefab structural insulated panels (SIP) can produce a highly energy-efficient structure.

The term 'self-build' is a fairly elastic one. While it does have connotations of going it alone, many self-builders rely heavily on other professionals to realize their building project. Some of the finest bespoke houses in the world are the results of a sympathetic partnership between client and architect.

An architect can offer a variety of services, from consultation and design to full supervision and project management, as detailed in 'The Practicalities', page 152. While architects have a breadth of expertise in many different areas which make them excellent troubleshooters for self-build projects, it is their creative input that is the focus of this section.

Unlike the designers attached to package-deal companies, architects do not come with any strings attached. You can commission an architect to do a feasibility study or come up with an original design, walk away with the result and build it yourself. This partial service is very attractive to self-builders who are happy to take over project management or work with a general contractor, but who need design input to translate dreams into reality.

It cannot be stressed too often that the most important prerequisite for a successful creative partnership is to find the architect or architectural firm that is on your wavelength. Architects tend to have some sort of design signature: they may have a resolutely contemporary approach, or a more traditional bent; they may be interested in the environmental impact of their designs or have expertise in working with a particular structural system. Look through magazines and the architectural press to see which recently published projects most appeal to you and are closest to what you are trying to achieve.

Whatever their individual design leanings, all architects are able to think spatially, which is something that nonprofessionals find hard to do. You may not find it difficult to read plans – although many people cannot quite get their heads round them – but chances are you will not have such refined instincts about what a particular space will feel like once it is built. A good architect will be able to think about the way different spaces relate to each other – that is, the progression or circulation from area to area – as well as issues to do with natural lighting and orientation, volume, scale and proportion, which will determine your house's ultimate spatial quality. The interplay of these factors can make all the difference between a serviceable but predictable house and one that offers a true sense of delight. Spatial quality of this kind is not necessarily dependent on spending more money: it can be something as unquantifiable as the way light plays along a corridor or spills down the stairs, or the views from level to level or from room to room. It tends not to be the sort of effect, however, that is gained accidentally: it is part of the creative thought that goes into a design.

Where architects also score highly is in the resolution of your requirements with the practical constraints imposed by your budget. Contrary to popular misconception, architects can save you money and help you make the absolute most out of limited space. If your budget is tight and your proposals are modest, architectural input can be just as valuable, if not more so, than if the sky's the limit. Where many particularly excel is in the design of fitted space, integrating servicing with storage so that your home functions smoothly and provides enough accommodation for your possessions.

LEFT: In many self-build schemes, architectural input is invaluable. Highly skilled at thinking spatially, in terms of volume as well as layout, architects can come up with solutions that deliver unexpected delight.

DESIGN AND BUILD

Such solutions often come from a lateral direction – for example, an architect might allow for a wider than standard hallway so that floor-to-ceiling cupboards can be built in, thus easing pressure on living areas and bedrooms.

The same principle is true when it comes to addressing the specifics of your site. By the time you have bought a piece of land, you may have come to know it very well, under different weather conditions and at different times of the day. Once you have involved an architect in your project, he or she will be able to proceed to work up a design that makes the most of the site's particular advantages and drawbacks. Again, a degree of lateral thinking may provide the solution to a problem which may not otherwise have been readily overcome. If, for example, you are building in a dense urban area, where overlooking and security are key issues, one approach can be to reverse the conventional house plan and place main living areas at the top of the house, where they will benefit from better daylight and more privacy, with bedrooms on the level below.

In addition, architects are generally well up to speed on the latest construction techniques, materials and finishes available. Your architect may be able to suggest an unusual finish you might not otherwise have considered and one that could also lead to considerable savings.

Or it may be that he or she is able to source standard materials and components in a more cost-effective manner than you can.

What no architect can do, however, is read your mind. You need to come prepared with a full brief and wish list of requirements, backed up with pictures, articles torn out of magazines or anything else which will start the creative ball rolling and give some indication of what you expect and want. Most importantly, you need to be absolutely clear about what you can afford to spend.

The design will evolve gradually, from initial sketch proposals right through to detailed drawings, if that is what you require. Keep the channels of communication open, and be prepared to say at any stage if proposals are deviating significantly from what you want. At the same time, do not automatically dig in your heels if the design seems to be heading in an unforeseen direction. Your architect should be able to justify every design decision, and there may be a very good reason why the plans are not quite as you expected. At the end of the day it is your house, but until handover it is very much the architect's house, too – it is far from surprising that there are many would-be self-builders in the architectural profession. Respect on both sides will go a long way to achieving a successful result.

ABOVE LEFT: Reversing the conventional house plan and placing a kitchen at the top level, where it benefits from toplighting, can be surprisingly successful.

ABOVE RIGHT: Increasingly, most people want their homes to have a good quality of natural light and easy connections with outdoor areas.

RIGHT: A dining table made of a single slab of marble is positioned directly under a sunroof that is operated by remote control.

The basic structure or shell of your home can be constructed in many different ways and in a range of materials from timber, brick and block, to steel. Each method and material, or combination of methods and materials, has its own set of advantages and disadvantages. Your choice will be governed by a number of factors, but is unlikely to be affected by matters of taste, as there is no particular reason why the structure needs to be expressed in overall style or elevational detail. Just by looking at a brick house, for example, you will not necessarily be able to tell whether it is masonry construction or whether the structure is actually made of timber, as is the case with many brick houses in the United States.

In areas where timber is plentiful and timber construction the norm, it can be simpler and cheaper to follow suit. In areas where solid construction is more typical, you may find building codes are unfavourably prohibitive when it comes to timber construction – for example, in some parts of the world, you are not allowed to use a timber structure for a house that is more than two storeys high, because of the perceived fire risk. Many of the anxieties concerning timber construction in Britain owe their origins to the Great Fire of London in 1666.

Foundations

The foundations are the basis of a building's structure, however that structure is composed or of whatever materials it is made. In many cases, there will not be much difference between the foundations required for solid construction and those for timber-frame, as the foundations will generally be determined by the ground conditions as much as by the weight of the structure that they support. In some instances, however, lightweight timber structures can be supported by more minimal pad foundations, causing less site disruption. Piling, for example, where foundations consist of individual concrete cores drilled and filled

at specific locations, may be chosen over strip foundations if the site is heavily wooded to avoid disruption to existing tree roots. Many eco houses, designed specifically to 'sit lightly on the land', have similarly minimal foundations. Although many self-builders attempt to do their own groundwork themselves, for the most part foundations are something best left to the professionals – it is heavy, messy work that requires quite specific skills.

The most common type of foundation is the strip footing, where trenches are dug under the position of the load-bearing walls, down to a frostproof depth, then filled with brick walling built on top of a bottom layer of unreinforced concrete. The required depth is specified in local building codes and obviously this depth varies according to climate. Deeper foundations are also required, naturally enough, if there is to be a basement.

In situations where a soil investigation has flagged up problems with the ground conditions, or where there are protected trees with root systems that impinge upon the footprint of your house, you will need specially designed foundations to get round the problem. This can add significantly to the cost of the build. Sometimes, however, problems only become obvious after the groundworks have got under way, which will entail going back the drawing board and coming up with a different way of tackling the foundations.

Foundations can be strengthened in various ways – by adding steel reinforcing bars or mesh, or by increasing the amount of concrete infill. More specialist foundations include piled foundations and raft foundations. Piled foundations require specialist equipment and a significant amount of expertise, but may be the only solution in certain soil conditions or where there is the need to fit round tree roots. Raft foundations, designed for use where there is ground movement, are also a job for the professionals to handle.

123

ABOVE: A contemporary use of stone facing in combination with sleek rendered concrete.

RIGHT: Timber infill softens the rather monumental quality of masonry construction.

Masonry construction

The dominant construction method in Britain and parts of Europe, excluding Scandinavia, is masonry or solid construction using brick and block, or less usually stone. While there are several different methods of solid construction, in all cases it is the brick or block walling that is the load-bearing element. In these structures, the weight of the roof rests on the external walls, which also support the floors that span between them, while the combined load of roof, walls and floors rests on the foundations. Some internal walls will also play a structural role; lateral stability and bracing are provided by floors and the roof.

The most usual form of masonry construction is cavity wall. In this method, the walling is composed of an outer skin, usually brick, and an inner wall made of some form of block, tied to the skin at intervals by wall ties. Between the two is a gap which prevents moisture from penetrating into the interior from the outer skin and which, equally importantly, serves as insulation. Depending on the type of cavity wall construction, the gap may be left unfilled or, more usually these days, filled or partially filled with insulating material. In cavity wall construction it is the inner wall, not the facing wall or skin, which is the load-bearing element. Different types of block are used to construct

this walling, some of which have insulating properties of their own, and price also varies widely. Unlike timber construction, where upper floors are always timber, masonry construction allows for solid floors at first and second levels, which enhances sound and thermal insulation. These are generally achieved using beams infilled with blocks.

Masonry construction is generally longer-lasting than timber structure and requires less maintenance over its life span. Cool in summer, warm in winter, houses built of brick and block have greater thermal mass than timber houses, which means they hold heat for longer and release it slowly, increasing energy efficiency. They are also easier to draughtproof and are inherently more soundproof.

On the downside, masonry construction is time-consuming, labour-intensive and more likely to be disrupted by bad weather, all of which may potentially increase your costs. If you choose to construct your house this way, you will not be able to use many prefabricated elements. Subsequent extensions or alterations that entail any structural changes will be more expensive and disruptive. Ecologically speaking, the use of brick and block construction is generally discouraged because of the high energy costs involved in the production and transportation of the materials.

Timber construction

Until fairly recently, timber construction was not viewed that favourably in Britain, a prejudice that lingered on centuries after the Great Fire. Previously advocates of this type of structure often found they had a struggle on their hands to gain the necessary approvals. This was despite the fact that there are many timber buildings still in existence which are centuries old. The increasing popularity of timber construction has improved matters considerably, as building control officers have become more familiar with it. One pioneer of timber-frame building in Britain was the architect Walter Segal, who was an important figure in the early days of the self-build movement. Now it is estimated that one in seven of all new homes in Britain employs some form of timber structure.

The situation is almost the polar opposite in the United States, where 90 per cent of domestic building is carried out using some form of timber structure, which is not surprising in a country where wood has always been a plentiful natural resource. In fact, timber construction is so prevalent that it can be difficult in some areas to find building workers who have masonry skills.

Timber construction is favoured by the eco-minded because materials come from renewable, sustainable sources and structures are easy to insulate. For self-builders, timber construction has also proved popular, as the structure generally goes up much faster and there is considerable scope for the use of prefabricated elements, which speeds the process further and reduces costs. Where prefabricated elements are not used, however, more accuracy may be required in construction. Wood also needs to be dried properly to avoid subsequent warping. Timber structures are noisier than masonry buildings, need greater maintenance and they lack the feeling of solidity that brick and block structures impart.

Within the broad category of timber construction, there are many different types of structure. The most basic is the traditional log cabin, where logs piled on top of one another form the load-bearing walls that support the roof. In recent years, this type of structure has made a comeback, aided by advances in material technology which allow for solid timber construction without the usual accompanying disadvantages of draughtiness and poor insulation values.

More common is the timber-frame or stick-build structure. Here, the structural skeleton of the building is formed by timber members, joists and rafters, with external and internal wall sheathing providing lateral stability. Many of these elements are standardized and can be prefabricated.

In yet another timber construction variant, structural insulated panels (SIPs) can be used as the main structural component. In

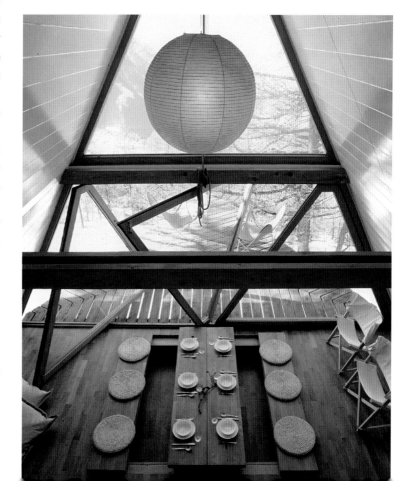

these 'stress skin' panels, it is the frame and sheathing together which provide the necessary strength for load-bearing; sections can be prefabricated in large sizes, fitted with insulation and may even have wiring and plumbing already installed. Many prefab houses rely on this type of structure. Naturally enough, construction is rapid and the need for skilled labour on site greatly reduced.

Finally, there is the method of post-and-beam construction, where the timber frame of columns, floor beams and joists and roof beams provide the entire structural support independent of any external or internal walls or partitions. The advantage of constructing this type of structure is that it allows for larger uninterrupted interior space. Only certain types of wood are suitable for use as structural members, including Douglas fir and oak. However, new types of engineered timber are now available, such as Paralam and Glulam, which consist of layers of weaker wood laminated under high pressure to create a material of great strength.

Steel construction

As it is generally a more expensive option than other building methods available, steel-frame construction tends not to be the first choice for self-build. However, there are some steel-frame kit houses on the market, and these might provide a more economical alternative.

The advantage of steel-frame is that the structures can be very light and minimal. Steel columns and beams, manufactured or pre-engineered to precision specification, do all the structural work and walls can be mere infills, even entirely glazed. The lightness and transparency is matched by open, free-form internal layouts where partitions can be placed anywhere or done without altogether. Steel frameworks can be engineered in work-shops and put together like a kit of parts on site in a matter of days.

ABOVE: This house was designed on a modular grid and features extensive glazing. The steel frame is the only coloured element.

RIGHT: Steel-frame structures, while expensive, can be quite light and minimal, which allows walls to be mere infills of glass.

ABOVE LEFT AND RIGHT:
The Wigglesworth-Till House in central London is built of a variety of unusual materials, including straw bale. One wing of the building is raised up on 'gambions', wire cages filled with lumps of recycled concrete.

RIGHT: Cocoon is a vacation house in Wye River, a small town in Victoria, Australia. Resembling an upturned boat or zeppelin, its interior is entirely clad in limewashed plywood. Two glass walls in the living area provide views of the ocean.

Unusual types of structure

Although it is the case that most self-build houses have structures which are either masonry or timber or a combination of the two, a small proportion of self-builders choose to build their own homes specifically to pioneer a particular structural method. Most of these, it would be fair to say, are motivated by ecological concerns.

Within this category fall mud or adobe houses, which can hardly be viewed as an eccentric alternative considering that one-third of the world's population lives in houses made in this way. In both adobe and rammed-earth construction, the raw ingredient is literally earth, either formed into bricks with the addition of sand, straw, cement or other binders, or tamped into forms where it sets hard. In Britain, traditional cob houses are constructed in a similar fashion.

Another unusual type of structure is that reliant on straw bales, in which compacted bales are used like building blocks. Stacked in staggered rows and secured with steel rods, they form load-bearing walls; alternatively the bales may be used as infill between another type of structural framework. Once the structure is complete, the bales are wrapped in wire and rendered with breathable stucco and plaster. In yet another departure, the 'Earthship', an eco housing form designed by American architect Mike Reynolds, has walls that are composed of tyres packed with earth and plastered over.

Naturally enough, you need to be especially dedicated to opt for a type of construction that falls outside the scope of standard building control. In order to get projects realized, many self-builders who have chosen to go an unusual constructional route have been forced to campaign to change local building codes, which tends to mean they have had to go out of their way to provide extra calculations and supporting evidence to prove structural soundness and fire-resistance, even if their proposals are in tune with an age-old vernacular. (For instance, just because adobe is the indigenous building style of certain parts of the southwestern United States does not mean that it is viewed favourably by local authorities.) Although this is a level of complication that many self-builders would prefer to avoid, if you are prepared to fight your corner and do your homework, you may well be successful. In the end, this will make the extra work you face worthwhile.

MATERIALS

ABOVE: A beautifully judged combination of materials – timber cladding and screens, rough-hewn stone and tile, steel frames and columns and glass – accentuate the lines and planes of the architecture.

132

A conversion of an existing property may set certain constraints on which materials you are able to use, particularly if that house dates back a century or more. When you build your own home, however, you have the opportunity to explore fully the wide range of options for surfaces and finishes, both externally and internally. Choice of materials has a huge impact on the design and character of a house.

Materials represent a significant amount of the cost of a build and their selection represents one of the few areas where a little creative manoeuvring can be done in terms of budgeting. You may not be able to reduce the

cost of foundations or the basic structure, but savings can be made by specifying or sourcing a cheaper material, say, for a kitchen counter, if there is an unforeseen cost overrun. Here it is a question of being hard-nosed about your priorities and long-term investment. It is always a bad idea to try to save money by specifying a substandard material or one that will wear out and require replacement sooner rather than later, particularly for surfaces such as floors, which are both dominant in their impact and disruptive to change at a later date. On the other hand, you may find it perfectly acceptable to live with cheaper, mass-market kitchen units and wait for the day when you have enough money to replace MDF doors with those of solid wood.

At the same time, always beware of over-specification, particularly if you find yourself changing your mind about a material once the build is under way. Try to resist the temptation to go for more expensive or luxurious finishes than you had first envisaged – it is a sure-fire way to end up seriously out of pocket.

Character and quality

Materials are the embodiment of spatial character; we relate to them immediately in a way that arouses all sorts of connotations and sensual responses. A room panelled in wood, for example, would feel, smell and sound very different to one where the walls are plastered. At the same time, we tend to associate rough-hewn natural surfaces and finishes with country living, while smooth, sleek materials such as glass and steel have strong urban and contemporary overtones. Then there is the perceived division between domestic materials and those more commonly found in public or industrial areas, as well as the notions of luxury embedded in rare or costly materials such as marble and stone.

Whatever your selection, try to think of ways of combining materials to give a sense of depth and character. An exposed brick wall can make a textural counterpoint in a room that is otherwise plastered, a shift of flooring material underfoot can signal a change of activity in an open-plan multipurpose space. Even the cheapest, most familiar material used in a wholehearted fashion can deliver an added fillip of interest.

Materials checklist
+ Ask yourself if the material in question is suitable for the specific application for which it will be used. Will it stand up to wear and tear? Will it stain or mark? How much maintenance will be required to keep it looking good? If it is to be used for flooring, is it resilient or will anything you drop break?

+ Are there any costs associated with its installation? Does it require specialist fitting? Do underlying surfaces require special preparation? The cost of a floor, for example, is not merely the amount you spend on the flooring itself, whether that is hardwood or carpet, but also includes the cost of fitting, underlay or subfloor preparation. Bear in mind, too, that some very heavy flooring materials cannot be laid over a timber subfloor, which won't support the weight.

+ What impact will the material have on the ambient character of your house? Materials that are transparent, translucent or reflective will enhance the quality of natural light; others are naturally darker and more enclosing. Acoustics are another significant factor: too many hard surfaces and your house will be noisy and rackety, with every sound uncomfortably amplified.

+ Is there an alternative material that would provide the same aesthetic and functional qualities, but be cheaper?

+ Is it possible to save money by buying the material from a second-hand outlet, such as a salvage yard? Or can the material be sourced more economically by investigating suppliers in different parts of the world?

+ If environmental issues are a priority, what is the environmental impact of the material? Does it come from a renewable source? What will be its effect on energy-efficiency?

+ If it is a priority that your house matches local buildings in style, can you use local materials to help it blend in?

+ Finally, how difficult is the material to get hold of? Will progress be delayed while you wait for a delivery? If you are reliant on a single far-flung supplier, you will have no room to manoeuvre if the company finds itself out of stock or if there is a protracted delay.

Wood

One of the most versatile of all building materials, wood has hundreds of applications. It has the added advantage that you can ensure it comes from a renewable, sustainable source, making it an environmentally sound option. Cost is dependent on species, with hardwoods such as oak generally being the most expensive, and engineered or manmade woods, such a plywood, OSB (oriented strand board) and hardboard being the cheapest. In all but the most manufactured form, wood has inherent liveliness and vitality, evident in the grain, as well as an appealing domestic quality.

Uses for wood

+ Structural elements, including timber members such as beams, columns and joists, or in the form of prefabricated trusses, stress skin panels and similar components.
+ Window and door frames and linings.
+ Architectural detailing, such as mouldings and trim.
+ External cladding and fascia.
+ Doors and cupboard and drawer fronts.
+ Flooring, either as a subfloor, an integral solid floor or a veneered covering.
+ Staircases, balusters and handrails.
+ Shutters and blinds, both internal and external.
+ Kitchen counters and vanity tops.
+ Shelving and other forms of built-in storage.
+ Wall panelling and cladding from tongue-and-groove boarding to thin veneered skins.
+ Handbasins and soak tubs.
+ Outdoor decking.

Points to consider

+ Make sure wood comes from a sustainable source. Certain species of tropical hardwood, such as mahogany and iroko, are endangered and should not be used unless you obtain them from a second-hand source.

+ If you cannot afford solid hardwood floors, softwood stained a suitable shade can make a good economical alternative. A decent grade of plywood, well sealed, can be a surprisingly practical floor in an area that does not see a lot of traffic.
+ Wood must be correctly seasoned before use or it will split and warp as it loses moisture content. Wood available from commercial timber merchants is generally predried to a moisture content of about 10 per cent, which is suitable for use in a centrally heated interior. You may, however, have to store the wood for a time in the area where it will subsequently be used, to allow for acclimatization.
+ Bamboo is a good alternative to solid wood and scores high in environmental friendliness. Bamboo flooring is as tough as oak; bamboo wall panelling and counters are also available.
+ If you are buying second-hand wood, such as old floorboards or parquet, make sure it is pest- and rot-free.

LEFT: Wood is a material with tremendous warmth and appeal, as well as an inherently domestic character. The veneered door fronts display the beauty of wood grain.
ABOVE: Many forms of architectural detail are traditionally made in wood, including balusters and handrails.

ABOVE: Brick comes in a range of colours and sizes. These dark engineered bricks have a contemporary edge.

RIGHT: Stone is an excellent material for bathroom use. These large slate tiles have been applied in staggered rows.

Brick and block

One of the fundamental elements in masonry construction, brick remains the preferred building material in many areas, if not for structure then at least for external cladding. Available in a range of earthy tones, bricks have a pleasing domestic scale and inherent textural interest. Blocks, on the other hand, are more utilitarian, and tend to be used where they will be subsequently covered up.

Uses for brick and block

+ Foundations, structural walling and load-bearing internal walls.
+ Fireplaces and chimneys, or to enclose built-in ovens.
+ Flooring in ground-floor areas.
+ External terracing and paths.
+ Thin brick 'slips' for wall cladding.

Points to consider

+ Bricklaying is a highly skilled trade and should not be taken for granted. You will need the services of a good bricklayer to ensure mortar joints are neatly executed.
+ Masonry construction is more prone to disruption from wet weather than dry forms of construction.

+ Second-hand bricks have a more natural, weathered appearance, but are often more expensive than buying new.
+ Brick floors can be laid in different patterns, from herringbone to basketweave.
+ For brick paths or terraces, choose paviors that are frost- and weather-resistant.
+ Be aware that local authorities may specify a particular type of brick to ensure your house conforms to local styles.

Stone

Because of its expense and relative scarcity, stone is not much employed in a structural capacity, although it is occasionally used as cladding. Nowadays, the chief application of stone is for interior surfaces and finishes, such as flooring or countertops. It remains very much a luxury material, however, and its cost can be prohibitive if you have a large area to cover. Stone – which includes limestone, slate, granite and marble – is incredibly varied in appearance, texture and finish. It also comes in different formats, from large, solid slabs to thin 'tiles' used for wall cladding. Finishes also vary widely, from highly polished surfaces, through matt textures, to more naturalistic rough-hewn surfaces.

Each type of stone has its own properties in addition to its own intrinsic character. Granite is very hard, typically flecked and comes in beautiful dark colours. It is often used as kitchen worksurfaces or vanity tops. The most typical use of slate – a dark, wavy stone that can be split or riven into thinner tiles – is as a roof covering, but slate flooring and wall tiling are also popular. Limestone is the most porous stone commonly used in the interior. It is typically pale, smooth and elegant-looking, although some additional protection in the form of dressings or seals is required if it is to be laid as a floor. Marble is supremely luxurious, whether it is employed as flooring or is being used as bathroom cladding.

ABOVE LEFT: Exposed stone walling makes an effective contrast to the sleek lines of a modern built-in kitchen.

ABOVE RIGHT: Concrete, once a byword for brutality, is now very popular as a final finish.

OPPOSITE ABOVE: Spiral staircases are commonly made out of metal. This example has textured treads to minimize slipping.

OPPOSITE BELOW: Metal surfaces are highly reflective and help to spread available light around a space.

Uses for stone

+ External cladding, cills and lintels.
+ Roof slates.
+ Fire surrounds, hearths and mantels.
+ Flooring.
+ Kitchen worktops and vanity tops.
+ Bathtubs and sinks.
+ Internal wall cladding.
+ Outdoor terraces and paving.

Points to consider

+ Installation is a professional job, requiring specialist skills, so you will need to hunt down a reputable and competent contractor.
+ Stone is heavy. Stone floors need to be laid over a stable, even concrete subfloor that can bear the weight.
+ Many types of stone, but most particularly limestone, are prone to staining and therefore require sealing.
+ It is advisable, even necessary, to choose rougher, textured finishes for stone flooring to prevent accidental slipping.
+ Stone has great thermal mass, holding heat and releasing it slowly. It can be very effective used over underfloor heating.
+ Artificial stone can be very realistic and is much cheaper and lighter than the real thing.

Concrete

Most houses, even the most environmentally friendly, have at least some concrete elements, most typically foundations. Lightweight concrete blocks are a standard building material and allow for more rapid construction than labour-intensive brickwork. In recent years, concrete has enjoyed something of a revival as an interior finish, both in the form of polished concrete floors or exposed concrete walls.

Uses for concrete

+ Foundations and footings, structural walls and interior load-bearing walls.
+ Subfloors, particularly on ground level.
+ Left exposed, polished, sealed or pigmented, concrete may serve as final finishes for walls and floors.
+ Because of its plasticity, concrete can be used to create curved interior partitions.

Points to consider

+ Laying concrete is a skilled job. Work will be delayed by bad weather.
+ Wet concrete causes severe burns and must be handled with care.
+ Its great thermal mass means concrete can be employed to increase energy efficiency.

Metal

The principal metal used in construction is steel, but a variety of others, from copper and brass to zinc and aluminium, also have applications as interior fittings, fixtures and finishes. Steel, while expensive, allows for structural minimalism, giving clear spans and open-plan interior space. Because steel has the highest embodied energy of all the materials used in building – around 300 times that of timber – its use can be problematic for those who are eco-minded. However, many metals, including steel, are readily recycled, which can offset the environmental drawbacks, as can the fact that steel is so strong that you do not need to use very much of it.

Uses for metal

+ Structural beams, columns and supporting frameworks.
+ Corrugated aluminium can be used for roofing, cladding or internally to make screens or enclosures.
+ Framing for windows or French doors.
+ Splashbacks, countertops and as a cladding for door fronts.
+ Metal treadplate can be used to create staircases and floors.
+ Wide range of applications for fixings and fixtures, from nails, screws and hinges to door handles and catches.
+ Sinks and bathtubs.
+ Radiators.

Points to consider

+ Salvage yards can be a good source of second-hand metal components, such as sinks, radiators or industrial-style fittings and fixtures.
+ Extensive metal surfaces can be chilly, noisy and clinical – they have a definite impact visually and in terms of ambience.
+ Stainless-steel counters require more upkeep than synthetic counterparts; brass fixtures are even more demanding in terms of maintenance.

139

Glass

In its vital role of admitting natural light to the interior, glass is an indispensable material. Depending on its specification, it can also be one of the most expensive. While glass lets in light, it also has a significant impact on ambient temperature. Large expanses of glass mean that rooms heat up uncomfortably on hot days and lose heat rapidly during cold weather. To counteract this, various different types of glass and glazing units have been developed, from double-glazed and triple-glazed units to low-E, or low-emissivity, glass. Low-E glass is coated with thin, transparent layers of silver oxide that reflect infrared energy back into the interior.

Uses for glass

+ All forms of glazing, including windows, French doors, fanlights, rooflights and glazed roofs.
+ Transparent internal screens and dividers.
+ Splashbacks and worksurfaces.
+ Glass bricks and blocks can be used to create interior partitions or as external infill.
+ Glass for stairs and flooring should be comprised of a 2cm (1in) top layer laminated to a 1cm (½in) base, with sandblasted friction bars to prevent slipping. It is generally used in metre-square panels.
+ Sinks and bathtubs.

Points to consider

+ Choose the right glass for its practical application, and take climate into account. If heat loss will be a problem, consider double-glazing or using low-E glass.
+ Be aware of safety and security. Toughened glass or laminated glass resists breakage and is much safer for French doors or any other application where accidents are more likely to happen.
+ Glass splashbacks, sinks and baths require constant maintenance to look good.
+ Small panels of tinted glass are a good way of adding vibrant colour.
+ Mirrored surfaces help to increase the sense of space in a small, enclosed area.

LEFT: A glazed balustrade on a mezzanine level within a double-height space provides minimal interruption of views and light from the huge windows.
BELOW: A vertical window provides a slice of a view from the tub.

Insulating materials

All new houses need to conform to specified standards of insulation as laid out in building codes and regulations. How well a roof or wall serves as an insulator is expressed as a U-value (heat transmission coefficient), with the lower the U-value the higher degree of insulation provided. This figure is calculated according to a formula that takes into account the degree to which each component within a structural element conducts heat. For example, to work out the insulation that is provided by a standard form of masonry construction, the cavity wall, the calculation of U-value takes into account the conductivity of the external brick, the air space, the insulating material itself, the interior brick or blockwork, and the plaster on top.

There are many different materials that can be used to insulate walls, floors and roof spaces. These include:

+ Mineral wool – stone wool or glass wool.
+ Polystyrene panels and foam.
+ Polyurethane panels and foam.
+ Polyester blanket.
+ Cellulose from recycled newspaper, either loose, sprayed or in panels.
+ Wood fibreboard.
+ Sheep's wool.
+ Flax, either in ropes or panels.

Decorating materials

From paint and wallpaper to leather, rubber, tile and mosaic, the range of decorating materials is truly vast, particularly when you take into account variables of pattern, colour and finish. Aside from taste and preference, your choice will ultimately be guided by what is left in your budget after the construction and basic fit-out is complete and the related issue of how much of the decorative work you intend to tackle yourself. Most people can make a decent job of painting, but other procedures, such as tiling, can be a different matter. If you are not sure you can do it yourself, do not attempt it. A badly tiled wall or floor will not affect the structural soundness of your house, but it will remain an all-too-visible eyesore.

Think about how long you expect the decoration to last. While it is no great chore to repaint a room every few years or so, you probably will want a floorcovering to last longer than that. Paying a little more for a durable material can be well worth the investment. Aside from questions of expense and practicality, another significant division to take into account is between materials that are natural in origin and those which are chiefly synthetic. Natural materials, as well as being more environmentally friendly, generally age better than artificial ones, which basically just degrade with wear.

RIGHT: The tight grid of mosaic tile makes a lively and practical surface in a bathroom. A glass sheet is fixed over the top of a vibrant red wall.

Environmental considerations may seem an optional extra for some self-builders, but others see such thinking as part of what good design should be all about. It is certainly true that a significant proportion of people who build their own homes do so out of a desire to live in a way that does as little harm to the planet as possible.

Even if you do not consider yourself to be an eco warrior, environmentally friendly design offers many other benefits. One of the most persuasive is reduced energy costs. The more energy-efficient your home is to run, the lower your bills will be. Many advocates of green living also maintain that natural, sustainable materials and environmentally friendly finishes make the home a much healthier place, where people are less likely to succumb to allergy-related illnesses and other disorders associated with exposure to chemicals and toxins.

Many so-called green alternatives, whether in terms of technology, constructional system or materials, are far more mainstream than they once were. Some lenders in the UK, for example, now offer solar mortgages which allow you to spread the considerable capital cost of installing solar roofs or panels over time, which brings this particular form of technology within the reach of a greater number of people. To an extent, one might also argue that the high standards of insulation that new houses are required to meet builds in a degree of environmental friendliness right from the start.

The newsworthy eco homes, built of straw bales, or with their own composting waste systems, may remain a minority enthusiasm. However, it is likely that as the world's natural resources of gas and oil begin to decline we will all have to start taking energy issues much

RIGHT: This energy-efficient weekend house in Switzerland is raised up on concrete posts so as to disturb the site as little as possible. Aside from the posts, the rest of the building is made of timber: pine for the structural frame with larch cladding.

ECO DESIGN

LEFT: Located in
the centre of Tucson,
Arizona, this eco-
friendly house
makes use of passive
solar strategies to
maintain comfortable
temperatures indoors.
The large overhang
shades the windows
from summer sun.
Walls are made from
well-insulated block.
Rainwater is collected
from the roof and used
to water the garden.

more seriously. A self-build project is by its nature building for the future and provides many different ways to address the increasing need for conservation and sustainability.

Siting

Eco design, like traditional building, adapts the house to suit its setting, in order to work with local climatic conditions. Such passive design strategies cost nothing but forethought, and can make a significant difference to ongoing energy requirements. At the same time, there is an emphasis on disrupting the site as little as possible by using structures that need only minimal foundations.

In cool climates, the aim is to site the house so that it benefits as much as possible from solar gain. In the northern hemisphere, this means orienting the design so the house faces south; if not due south, then at least within a margin of 20 degrees east or west. The south-facing side should comprise up to 60 per cent window and the north-facing side should have minimal openings. To guard against overheating in the summer months, there should be large overhanging eaves to act as a sunbreak. As warm air rises, locating living areas on the top or first floor will make the most of solar gain instead of it being wasted on areas of the house not used during the day, as will the use of materials with high thermal mass, such as concrete, stone and brick, which warm up slowly during the day and release heat gradually overnight. A compact plan is also more energy-efficient than a design which is of irregular shape. Earth-sheltering, where the house is partially dug into an earth bank or slope, uses the high thermal mass of the earth to retain the heat from the sun.

In hot climates, the aim is to keep the house as cool as possible without resorting to artificial means. Openings should be aligned with prevailing winds for through-breezes, and kept small and minimal on the side of the house

that faces the sun. Additional sun screening can be provided by overhanging eaves, climbing vegetation, verandas and brises-soleils. Low buildings that enclose open courtyards are inherently cooler because there is more surface area from which heat can be lost and patterns of cross-ventilation are facilitated. Courtyard pools cool the air further.

Insulation

In cold climates, insulation is one of the most effective and cheapest ways of improving energy-efficiency. Without proper insulation, no matter how efficient or sophisticated your heating system, half of the heat that system produces will escape through walls, windows, roof and possibly the floor if the house has a basement or is set above the ground, which is a phenomenal waste of money and resources. As well as ensuring that you build in a high degree of insulation into walls, roof voids, ground floors and around water tanks and pipes, you should also try to make any openings as draughtproof as possible. Tight-fitting windows and doors reduce heat loss. Double-glazed or triple-glazed units, or the use of low-E glass, also have high insulating properties.

Unfortunately, the most efficient insulating materials tend to be those which, like mineral wool, polyurethane and polystyrene, are the least environmentally friendly. One popular green choice is to utilize insulation made of recycled newspaper.

Energy-efficient heating systems and appliances

Choose energy-efficient heating systems and appliances to minimize energy use. Modern boilers and control systems are much more efficient than previous models. Condensing boilers reclaim heat from exhaust gases and can achieve efficiency ratings of 90 per cent when combined with some form of electronic control that adjusts heat production to match

ABOVE: 'A House for the Future', designed by Jestico and Wiles, is a prototype for sustainable housing which can be visited at the Museum of Welsh Life in Cardiff. Every element, from the turf roof to the choice of materials and energy supply, has been informed by the principles of environmental construction and sustainability.

your pattern of consumption. Many of these systems are more expensive than standard ones, but the investment is a sound one as it is paid back over time in lower fuel bills.

Cookers, stoves, refrigerators and freezers consume the most energy after central heating or cooling systems. Look out for models with good energy-efficiency ratings.

Alternative sources of energy

A more active way of saving energy is to harness the free, clean, renewable energies of the sun and wind. For most people, benefiting from wind power is most likely to be achieved by signing up to a green energy provider. Solar power, on the other hand, can more readily be generated on an individual basis, although the costs are currently quite high.

Solar technology has certainly improved in leaps and bounds over the past few years and has become much more affordable, although

you do have to take the long view and think in terms of a payback period of decades rather than years. A solar mortgage, a service offered by some providers, can help to spread the cost so you do not have to find a large capital sum at the outset. New photovoltaic systems use silicon cells to convert radiant solar energy into electricity which can be stored for later use. These cells may be grouped in panels which are installed on a roof, or alternatively can be in the form of tiles and slates that comprise the roof itself. The systems require specialist design and careful siting.

Conserving water

Eco design is concerned as much with water conservation as it is with energy-efficiency. Water consumption can be dramatically reduced by simple strategies such as showering rather than bathing, choosing to install low-flush toilets and fitting flow regulators to taps

(faucets) and showerheads. It is also possible to design roofs to facilitate the collection of rainwater for garden irrigation.

Those dedicated to self-sufficiency might opt for a greywater system that filters mildly soiled water from washing, showering or bathing, and uses it to flush toilets or for watering the garden. These systems, which run off greywater through coarse gravel, then through reed beds, are only practicable if you have a significant amount of land – an average urban back garden will not provide enough space for this option, unfortunately.

Waterless waste disposal can be achieved with composting toilets, which collect waste in a large sealed container where it is broken down over a period of months into harmless compost, which you can then utilize on your garden. The installation of composting toilets is governed by local codes, and it is not permitted in some areas.

Choosing materials and finishes

The selection of materials and finishes has obvious implications for the environment. However, it is not always easy to evaluate the relative merits of one particular material over another. The issues involved can be complex.

Just to take one example, wood is a material that is widely acknowledged to be environmentally friendly. It is renewable, it is biodegradable and it comes from a living source that cuts levels of carbon dioxide in the atmosphere. However, many species of tree are now endangered, including mahogany and teak, and deforestation, particularly in tropical rainforests and in ancient old-growth forests in temperate regions, has had a severe impact both on local communities and on indigenous plants and wildlife. Where wood is harvested, then transported halfway across the globe, the associated energy costs are high. What is

ABOVE: A range of eco-friendly materials and finishes have been used throughout this New Zealand house, including bamboo on the ceiling, tatami mats on the bed platform and cork tiles on the floor.

149

LEFT: This beautifully
articulated timber
staircase made of
locally felled pine
is a distinctive feature
of an eco treehouse
in the Kwazulu-
Natal midlands of
South Africa.
BELOW: Bamboo is an
excellent alternative
to hardwood.

more, where wood is treated with chemicals to improve fire- and pest-resistance, its healthful properties are compromised.

One significant consideration you should always factor in when weighing up alternative materials is the concept of embodied energy. This is the sum of all the energy that is required to produce the material in question: its harvesting or the extraction of its raw ingredients, subsequent transportation to the factory where it is processed, the act of processing itself, the transportation of the finished material to where it will be used, and the amount of energy that is used during its installation or construction.

As far as construction materials are concerned, many eco-minded self-builders opt for some form of timber structure. Others explore the further reaches of alternative technology, choosing to build in rammed earth or straw bale.

Strategies for choosing environmentally friendly materials

+ Avoid any material that comes from an endangered source, such as old-growth timber and endangered hardwoods. Make sure wood comes from an approved sustainably managed plantation, as certified by the Forestry Stewardship Council or similar bodies.
+ Make a conscious choice to utilize local materials wherever possible and practicable to minimize energy costs in transportation.
+ Try to use reclaimed or salvaged materials or those which contain a significant recycled content rather than opting for brand-new.
+ Seek out materials that are durable so that they require less frequent replacement.
+ Use natural materials such as bamboo, cork, paper, linoleum and terracotta tile instead of synthetic and highly processed ones such as various forms of manufactured wood, rubber, vinyl, and most types of ceramic tile.
+ Avoid plastics as much as you can in addition to glues, seals and other finishes that contain plastics such as epoxy resin and formaldehyde.
+ Choose natural or casein paints, linseed or tung oil and beeswax for interior finishes, sealing and decoration.
+ Remember that clay plaster is not industrially processed like gypsum plaster and can be left unpainted and unsealed, which is an aid in breathing wall construction.

151

ECO DESIGN

This section gives a summary of all the practical issues you need to address to build your own home. Firstly, you need to come up with a brief that grounds your plans in reality. Then, there's the question of financing, not to mention finding that elusive site. Also included in this section is an introduction to official permissions and regulations, as well as a guide to the various design and construction options open to you, from full architectural service to going-it-alone.

THE PRACT

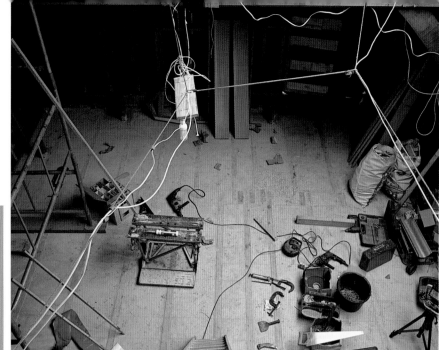

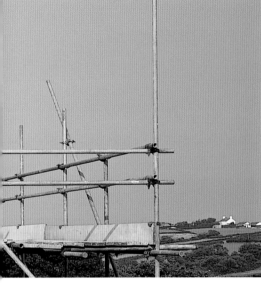

ICALITIES

THE BRIEF

If your castle in the air is going to become a built reality, you need to set parameters. By now, you should have an idea of what you are trying to achieve, whether it is an eco-friendly cabin in unspoilt countryside or a modernist urban infill. The next stage is to come up with a brief.

A brief grounds dreams and ideas in reality by setting reasonable limits on your expectations. It can serve as a personal plan of action or the beginning of a design dialogue with a qualified professional. Either way, it is invaluable.

Budget

The most important parameter to set in place is your budget. Good budgeting does not just mean setting a financial ceiling and sticking to it. It entails assessing priorities, choosing the right methods and materials – and even a certain degree of lateral thinking.

With a bit of luck, if you budget correctly, you will spend only what you can afford and no more. In addition, you will end up with a house that has a market value equal to or exceeding the investment you put into it. The last point is important. Even if you can afford to spend X amount of money on a build, if you are not going to get the same return at the end of the day, you will effectively be out of pocket.

At the most basic, a budget breaks down into the cost of the land and the cost of construction, which in turn is a factor of the size of the house you intend to build, its specification and how much of the work you intend to tackle yourself. Building costs are regularly published and updated in self-build magazines, which will enable you to compare different options. If you have your heart set on a particular location, then the land cost will be a more or less fixed element. If you are open-minded about where you want to live, you will have more flexibility in your financial planning.

It is generally recommended that the land cost should represent about one-third of the eventual value of your new house and the building costs another third, while the remainder should represent equity or profit. That is the theory. In reality, land values vary widely, which means that this cost may represent anything from a quarter to half of the eventual value. Building costs are generally more stable, but these, too, fluctuate a little, often between urban areas and rural areas, or between work carried out during a busy season or in quieter periods.

Where the figures just do not add up, you will have to look at your plans again. Reconsidering location, reducing projected size of the accommodation, removing expensive fixtures, servicing systems or materials from your wish list and tackling more of the work yourself are all ways of bringing costs in line. (See also Financing on p 157.)

Know your limits

Construction costs vary according to how much of the work you do yourself. Many self-builders limit themselves to an organizational role, and leave everything else to the professionals. Others like to roll up their sleeves and get stuck in, learning on the job if necessary. The hands-on approach is undoubtedly satisfying and is all part of the appeal of building your own home. But you have to be realistic about how much you can do. In almost all cases, you are going to need outside help for at least some of the work.

It is important from the outset to have a clear understanding of your own capabilities. If you have always been a practical person and have a number of relevant skills – perhaps you enjoy woodworking or tiling, or have a basic knowledge of plumbing – you stand a much better chance of saving money by taking on more of the physical work. Aside from a basic level of manual skill, you will need plenty of patience and stamina, and enough free time to devote to the project. Doing it yourself will not save you money if you have to take unpaid leave from your job and your salary exceeds what you would have otherwise paid a builder.

During the course of a self-build project many people are surprised by the number of new skills they pick up and how much satisfaction that gives them. Others who have overestimated their skills or underestimated the complexities of the work in question quickly get into hot water. If you have never been a particularly practical person, chances are you will not suddenly turn into one now. It can cost you a fortune when you ruin materials, take twice as long to finish a job as a professional would or compromise the integrity of the project with substandard work. If you are all thumbs practically speaking, but have a good head for organization and detail, you can still bring down construction costs by running a project on a subcontract basis, hiring the necessary tradespeople directly.

Assessing your needs

The final part of the brief is understanding what your requirements are and where your priorities lie. Before you consider a particular design approach or consult an architect, work out what you want to achieve. Draw up a wish list and think hard about which items on it are essential, which would be preferable and which would be the icing on the cake. Be prepared for your partner and the rest of your family to have their own sometimes very firm ideas!

At this stage of the game, try to avoid having fixed ideas about design and overall style. Focus more on the way you live or ideally want to live, as well as the functions that you expect your new home to fulfil.

Size How much accommodation do you require? Size has a direct bearing on construction costs. Many people are attracted to self-build because it is a cheaper means of gaining a bigger house than buying an existing one in the same location. If space per se is a prime consideration, this is not an area in which you will necessarily want to compromise. If other factors are more important than floor area, you may be able to cut costs by reducing the projected size of your build. Remember that spatial quality is not always a function of size – in other words, bigger is not always better. A large house can also have greater ongoing costs in terms of heating and maintenance.

Related issues, particularly when it comes to resale value, include the size of individual rooms and numbers of bedrooms. A good-sized kitchen, with space enough to eat in, is the single biggest selling point of any house. You can do without a separate dining room without losing resale value as long as the kitchen and living room are big enough. Think, also, about the number of bedrooms and their respective sizes. A house that has a greater number of smaller bedrooms will always have a greater market value than a house that has fewer, more generously proportioned ones. This is not to say that you should not opt for the accommodation that you want – merely that you should be aware of market preferences and take these into consideration.

Timescale How long do you expect to stay in your new house? If this is your dream project and you anticipate spending the rest of your life in your home, think about how your needs might change over the years so that you build in enough flexibility to accommodate shifts in lifestyle. If you expect to move on within a shorter time frame, you need to make doubly sure you will recoup your investment. Resale value can be adversely affected by designs that the market views as eccentric or too individual.

Function Think carefully about all the functions you will require your new home to fulfil. Aside from providing accommodation for basic everyday activities such as living, eating and cooking, bathing and sleeping, what other functions need to be accounted for? Do you want to include a fireplace or stove as a focal point of the living area? Do you want a separate utility room, or will you include your laundry machines in the kitchen or a bathroom? How many bathrooms do you require? Do you want a separate shower room or toilet? En suite bathrooms are both practical and desirable market features, while additional washbasins can ease bottlenecks in family routines. And what about servicing? Do you want underfloor heating or a central vacuum system, for example?

If you run your own business you may find it cost-effective to include a work unit as part of your new build. In some areas, this can make proposals more acceptable to local authorities, as well as saving you money in the long term if you are presently renting office or business space. New-build also provides the opportunity to take into account storage requirements in a wholehearted fashion. Older housing stock can be particularly lacking in this respect. Built-in storage and storage rooms such as dressing areas can make a huge difference to the ease with which you tackle everyday routines. Another element to consider is the balance between house and garden. Is outdoor living or a big garden a priority, or are you prepared to do with less outdoor space in order to maximize room sizes?

Then there is a question of planning for future needs. Do you want to incorporate a self-contained granny apartment or an attic or basement that could be converted for teenage use at a later date? Is it important for you to have a garage?

Expression Building your own home gives you the opportunity for creative expression. You do not have to be an architect or designer to have some idea about the type of property that appeals to you. Are you a traditionalist or in search of something more cutting edge? Are there particular materials to which you are drawn? Are you happier with conventional room-by-room layouts or are you attracted by the potential of open-plan flexible spatial arrangement? Lighting, both daylight and artificial, also has a big impact on architectural character and atmosphere. You might want to consider top lighting from skylights if you are keen on creating an airy, uplifting mood in living areas.

It is well worth taking the time to assemble a cuttings file of houses featured in magazines that particularly appeal to you – not just interiors, but also exteriors and details. This can be useful when it comes to discussing design issues with architects and other professionals.

Are you expecting to move your existing furniture and furnishings into your new home, or are you intending to start again from scratch? Which pieces of furniture could you not be parted from? One or two antiques can work perfectly well in a modern setting, but if your furniture consists entirely of period pieces, it will require a context that is more sympathetic in terms of architectural detail.

Location Some self-builders are tied, either by preference or by their career, to a specific location. This is naturally somewhat limiting, especially if you are trying to build in a city or a sought-after area. You will invariably find that sites are going to be scarce and, when you do find one, it will be relatively expensive and possibly problematic. If location is not an issue, you will be able to cast your net further afield, possibly even as far as another country. If you are thinking about building abroad, it is important to gain an idea of how cultural, bureaucratic, legal and language differences will affect the running of your project. You stand a better chance of success if you are already familiar with the area and can make yourself understood in the language.

Eco-friendliness New houses provide the opportunity to build in eco-friendliness from the outset. Many self-builders rate this as a priority out of conviction or principle. Even if you have not previously considered yourself as particularly environmentally aware, this is still a good time to consider the long view. Energy costs are set to rise as the world's stocks of oil and gas decline. If you intend to remain in your new house for the conceivable future, it makes sense to investigate ways of making it as energy-efficient as possible, if not for the sake of your conscience, then at least for the sake of your long-term financial security. You may be prepared to spend the extra money to install solar slates or panels, knowing that you will remain in your house for the time it takes for the investment to pay for itself. Alternatively, you can look for more passive ways of making your home as energy-efficient as possible through its orientation, for example, or by making sure that it is highly insulated.

Finally A brief is like a gestation process. Spend as long as it takes thinking about the various options and what you really require. At the same time, expect your ideas to evolve. This will start to happen as soon as you find your site and enter into discussions with design professionals.

FINANCING

Raising the money for a self-build project is much easier and more economical than it used to be. In the past, lenders were reluctant to provide a mortgage before bricks and mortar were in place. That left self-builders with the rather expensive option of selling their original property in order to buy the land, renting accommodation for the period of construction and meeting construction costs with a combination of whatever equity was left over and expensive bridging loans secured against the value of the land. When the house was built, the loans would then be repaid by a standard mortgage.

When self-build mortgages first came on the market, they addressed this problem by advancing money at the end of agreed stages of the build, so that the entire loan (and interest) was not carried throughout the period of construction. New self-build mortgages are better still and provide even greater financial advantages.

Sources of funds

If you already own a property, the immediate funds available to you will consist of whatever savings or investments you already have, together with the equity you have in your present home. That may well be enough to finance your project. If that is the case, you will only need short-term financing for the construction period. If you do not own a property, or have insufficient resources to buy a site and cover the construction costs, you will need a self-build mortgage.

Self-build mortgages

The self-build mortgage allows you to draw down funds in stages as and when you need them, so you pay the minimum of interest while your house is being built. Previously, self-build mortgages only released funds once an agreed stage of the build was completed. This still left some self-builders out of pocket. Those who did not have enough cash up front to finish a stage of construction were forced to sell their existing property or arrange expensive loans. Another disadvantage was that lenders would release funds only when a construction stage had been inspected and passed by their own surveyor, adding extra unwanted pressure to scheduling.

New self-build mortgages address the problem of cash flow by providing funds in advance, rather than on completion of a stage. This has particular benefits for those who are opting for kit homes or timber-frame construction because companies who provide such products require payment up front. And there are many other advantages besides.

The amount that can be borrowed is as high as 95 per cent of the cost of the land and 95 per cent of the cost of the construction. That means you can secure your site with a relatively small deposit and without having to sell your existing home to release the equity. You can also carry on living in your existing home while you build your new one, provided you can service both mortgage payments. With cash available when you need it, you are then able to shop around for the best prices for materials and labour.

A wide range of self-build mortgage products are now available, including fixed rate, capped rate, tracker and discounted. As is the case with all mortgages, the bank or lender has to be satisfied that your income can support repayments. The ratio of loan to income varies, but it is generally two and half times a joint income and three to four times a single income. In the case of some self-build mortgage packages, income is defined as what you have left after you have paid your existing mortgage.

In addition, the lender will need to see detailed plans and proposals, backed up with proper cost estimates. Include in your proposed budget the cost of professional fees, insurance and warranty premiums, any taxes payable on the land purchase, a generous margin for contingency, cost of rented accommodation for the construction period (if it is necessary to sell your home to finance the build) and the financial cost of borrowing itself. In Britain and Europe, there are special arrangements for self-builders when it comes to reclaiming VAT. If you buy your own materials, you can often reclaim the VAT you paid, which can give you a saving of nearly 20 per cent.

Remember that you stand a better chance of coming out of the whole exercise in good financial health if you are realistic about what you can afford. Err on the side of caution, particularly if the housing market in your area is going through a period of volatility. The last thing you want is to finish your build and find you cannot sell your previous property for what you had thought it would fetch or, worse still, find that you cannot sell your property at all.

In the same way, do not plan to spend your entire budget on the build. Build in a substantial margin – up to 10 per cent of the total cost of the scheme – as a contingency allowance. This is your financial safety net in case something goes wrong.

Insurance

No matter how well you are prepared, or how smoothly the whole build seems to be going, bad things can happen out of the blue. A storm that may lift only a few tiles from the roof of your existing house might seriously batter the one that you have under construction. Materials or tools might be stolen from your site. A third party

might suffer damage to their property or injury to their person. Insurance is vitally important for all self-builders, even if the work is being carried out as a single contract with a building firm that has its own insurance cover.

A self-build insurance policy should cover the following:
+ **Public liability** This insures you against any claim made by a third party whose property or person is damaged or injured as a result of your building work. Bear in mind that you are still liable even if someone has trespassed on your site and hurt themselves in the process.
+ **Employer's liability** This covers you against any accidents which subcontractors or others that you employ may have when working on your site.
+ **All risk** This covers you against fire, theft, flood, storm and acts of vandalism.

Warranties

Your lender may not insist on self-build insurance – it is up to you to put that essential cover in place. But a lender may well insist on a building warranty. Warranty schemes provide a means by which work in progress can be inspected and certified as passing an acceptable standard. If, after your house is finished, a failure occurs that is down to faulty workmanship, the warranty also provides cover to put things right. Lenders insist on warranties to guarantee that they are not offering a mortgage on what will turn out to be a substandard property. If you do not need a mortgage, you might still need a warranty in the

future if you decide to sell the house and the new owners require one to secure their own mortgage.

There are various types of warranty schemes available to self-builders. Some are run by national building organizations. Alternatively, you can hire an architect to inspect the site at agreed stages and certify that the work has been carried out satisfactorily.

FINDING LAND AND SITE EVALUATION

Finding a site is the first big step in self-build. Before you go in search of a piece of land, try not to have too many fixed ideas about the eventual design and style of your house beyond the basic parameters established in your brief. Tracking down land in your preferred location can be fraught enough. Matching a dream house to a dream site makes the task infinitely more difficult. Potential sites can have their idiosyncrasies – some slope, some are wooded, some are small – and others are downright problematic. To a large extent, how these are resolved or overcome will define the design process.

Land, like most other things that are bought and sold, is valued according to the laws of supply and demand. In most cases, sites in remote rural areas are cheaper and easier to find than slices of land in the middle of dense urban centres or in a picturesque spot in the commuter belt. If the ease of finding land varies from area to area, it also varies from country to country. In countries such as the United States, where construction of individual new houses is long-established, finding land is much simpler than it is in Britain, for example, where new building in previous decades has been more commonly carried out by commercial developers. Difficult, however, does not mean impossible. According to the National Council of Mortgage Lenders, self-build is currently the fastest-growing sector of the British property market, accounting for one in three of all new detached houses built every year – bigger than any single commercial developer. Those sites are out there somewhere.

As far as possible, make it easier for yourself by keeping an open mind about location. If you are prepared to widen your net you may find a site more quickly – you might even find several from which to choose. At the same time, do not expect perfection. Most, if not all, sites will present one or two drawbacks. If resolving these will not entail huge expense or unacceptable compromise, accept the fact that 'good enough' is better than nothing at all. Still, it is also important to be aware that some sites on the market present just too many problems to be feasible options. These should be left well alone. See Site evaluation on page 160.

Where to find land

On the Internet Cyberspace allows you to hunt for land in every corner of the globe without having to venture from the comfort of your home. Some site-finding agencies charge a subscription for their services. A plus with Internet listings is that they are likely to be more up to date than those published in magazines. The Internet can also provide you with an indication of which agents deal in land.

In the press Land is offered for sale in the classified pages of local newspapers, in self-build magazines and sometimes even in the national press. Private sales are very often advertised in local papers.

On foot Whether you are looking for land in your own area or in another location altogether, getting out and about can be a good way of tracking down a site. In cities, many sites that are too small to develop commercially but are large enough for a single house can be found tucked away in 'backlands' locations behind or between other houses. Redundant commercial premises – such as yards, old workshops and storage depots – can also be promising building sites, particularly in areas where the authorities look favourably on change of use. Do not be put off by superficial dereliction – junk, broken-down sheds and undergrowth can always be cleared. Equip yourself with a detailed map and look for unexplained gaps or portions of land with unspecified uses. If it is not clear who actually owns the land, try a Land Registry or title search to find your answer.

Under an existing house In many areas, it is possible to tear down an existing building and put up a new one. This is obviously more cost-effective the more dilapidated the existing house or building – unless you have money to burn, buying a perfectly decent house to get your hands on the land it is sitting on is far from an economical option.

In a site development In the United States, and increasingly in Europe, individual sites are being offered by companies which have bought up tracts of land for subdivision, then put in access roads and servicing. An overall development strategy will usually have been agreed, specifying suitable sizes and house types.

With others Get to know other self-builders and you may find that someone has found land that is too big for a single house, but would be ideal for two or three.

At an estate agent's or realtor's In many areas of the world, local agents have a selection of sites on their books. In Britain, however, agents often tend to have ongoing relationships with builders, architects and developers, which means that private individuals are less likely to hear about a site that has come up.

At auction Plots of land are regularly auctioned. Agents and vendors often prefer to auction land because it can be harder to put a correct market value on an undeveloped site than to place a value on an existing property. Auctions, however, are not for the faint-hearted or for those who have had no experience in this type of transaction. You need to be absolutely certain that it is the site you want and that there are no hidden problems, or you may find yourself owning a piece of land you cannot build on.

At your local planning department Check the register of current planning applications. In Britain, an application for 'outline' permission indicates that the site's owner is seeking to enhance its market value; it does not necessarily mean that the owner intends to build on the land. A site with proposals that have been submitted for 'detailed' permission is less likely to be for sale.

At your local council or utility board Local authorities, utilities and rail companies sometimes have plots of land for disposal.

In your own backyard If your present house has a large garden and there is the potential to create street access, your search may be over.

Site evaluation

You can count yourself truly lucky if you find a site that matches all your criteria in your chosen location and at a price you can afford. Most self-builders find they have to compromise and accept a site that meets most but not all of their requirements. Some people find they are prepared to pay a bit more; some may accept a smaller site; others may reconsider location.

Once you have found a site, and before you go ahead and snap it up, you must evaluate all the conditions thoroughly to establish whether it is practical or even possible to build on the land. Most people know what to look for when it comes to buying a house. Buying land is a very different proposition – you may need specialist advice. If you buy a piece of land, then discover that it is contaminated or local zoning or planning regulations do not permit residential development, the only way you will get your money back is to sell to someone else who has not done their homework either.

Planning status

It is not advisable to buy a site that does not have some form of planning consent for residential use. In the United States, zoning ordinances, as part of local development plans, specify which lots are for residential development and which are intended for commercial use. With respect to residential development, a wide range of other stipulations, from plot size to building height, will also be laid down.

If you are buying a site in Britain, make sure that it has at least 'outline' planning consent. Do not steam ahead and count on getting permission later, as you may end up owning land you cannot build on. You do not have to own a plot to apply for planning permission. If the site you want to buy does not already have planning permission, you can make purchase conditional on gaining consent.

The planning history can indicate whether or not you are likely to meet local opposition to your proposals. A thick file stuffed with letters from neighbours objecting to development on the grounds of overlooking or loss of light may well indicate you will have a struggle on your hands to win hearts and minds. Or it could simply show that the previous applicant did not try hard enough to explain their proposals.

While investigating planning status, it is worth finding out whether there are significant proposals, public or private, for the area surrounding your site that would compromise your own development by blocking light and views, increasing noise and traffic, or causing any similarly detrimental effect. As soon as that airport, supermarket or motorway is built, your quality of life will decline as abruptly as your home's value. See also Permissions and regulations, page 162.

Access

To develop a piece of land you need clear rights of access to it. Many residential sites offered for sale in the United States already have access roads and service connections put in place by a land developer. In Britain, that is still rarely the case. Access can be a complicated issue and you may need the services of a solicitor to determine the precise legal position. Do not assume just because there is a lane, alley or road leading to the site that you will be entitled to use it once you have bought the land.

If there is a clear right of access, think about how easy or difficult it will be to use. Is there enough space to park and turn a car? Will delivery vehicles be able to bring materials and equipment to the site, or will these have to be unloaded some distance away? Is the access road steep, which could cause problems in severe weather? Is it an unsurfaced road that will require paving and add to your costs?

Services

Another important consideration is the ease with which service connections can be made. Some sites are already serviced; many are not. You need to find out whether connections to main services – drainage, water, electricity, telecommunications, gas – are both possible and cost-effective. In rural areas, where routing pipework to hook up with main drains may prove too expensive, you will need to consider drainage into a septic tank or some other form of sewage disposal. In really remote locations, your house may need to be fully self-sufficient in terms of sewage, water and power generation.

Also find out whether cabling, gas mains, drains or water mains already cross your site. Sometimes that makes it easier for you to make your own connections. In other circumstances, where an 'easement' on the title deed rules out construction over the drain or cabling, your site will be virtually unusable unless you are prepared to go to the expense of diverting servicing.

Site specifics

If there are no outstanding drawbacks, you may wish to go on to commission a site survey and possibly a soil survey. Vendors' plot details can be imprecise and may even be misleading. A survey will provide you with exact dimensions, boundaries, levels and position of site features such as trees which may limit options for siting and design.

+ Does the site receive sunlight or is it shaded by surrounding buildings and trees?
+ Is it in a sheltered location or exposed to high winds?

+ Are there trees on the site or immediately adjacent which might affect the siting or the design of foundations? Are they protected by a preservation order?
+ Is the site in a conservation area or any area designated as of special scientific or historic importance?
+ Does the site slope excessively?
+ What are the ground conditions like? Will the subsoil support conventional foundations? Is the site waterlogged, ruling out a basement and possibly meaning expensive foundations?
+ Are there views you would like to enhance or screen? How noisy is the surrounding area?
+ Is the site located in an area that is prone to flooding or cliff erosion?
+ Has the site been contaminated or polluted through industrial use?
+ Is this site located in an area that has a prevalent building style that might influence planners' attitudes? If so, what are the cost implications?

Legal advice

The sale of land is highly regulated and legalities vary from country to country. One thing is certain: once you have found your site you will need the services of a solicitor, lawyer or relevant legal professional to handle the sale for you, just as you would if you were buying a house. Ideally, your solicitor should check through the title deeds thoroughly before you enter any contractual arrangement or hand over a deposit. He or she should also be able to confirm the precise planning status. Fees for this service vary as much as rules and regulations, so make sure you look into this first.

PERMISSIONS AND REGULATIONS

Regulations governing the use, construction and siting of new buildings vary from country to country and region to region. Despite local variations, these broadly fall into two categories. The first addresses use of the land and how that use will impact on the surrounding area and local economy. The second type is concerned with the structure itself and whether work meets specified standards of soundness and safety.

If you use an architect, he or she will be able to negotiate permissions on your behalf. If not, it is up to you to find out what is officially required and negotiate the hurdles.

Planning permission and zoning

In Britain every local authority has its own development plan which regulates the way that land is used in the different areas under its jurisdiction. Some parts of a borough, for example, may be regarded as suitable for industrial or commercial development, while others will be designated for residential or mixed use.

There are several stages in the planning process. The first is to make sure that you can build a house on the site at all. If your site has outline permission for development, you can go on to draw up detailed proposals and submit these for 'detailed' or 'full' planning consent. If the site you propose to buy does not have outline permission, you have two options. Either you can walk away from purchase and look elsewhere, or you can apply for permission and make the sale contingent on gaining it. You do not need to own a site to apply for planning permission. Pay a visit to your local planning office and talk to an officer about what is likely to be permissible.

If the site was previously used for commercial or light industrial purposes and is still designated as such you will need to apply for change of use. The local planning officer will be able to give you some idea of whether or not this will be awarded. Where a local authority is endeavouring to maximize employment possibilities in the area and where the surrounding neighbour-hood remains largely commercial or industrial, change of use is unlikely to be given. If the surrounding area is now predominantly residential or if you can demonstrate that there is a 'live-work' element to your proposals, you may well be successful in your application for change of use.

Once you have obtained outline consent, the next stage is to submit detailed proposals showing site layout, floor plans and exterior elevations, and specifying which materials you intend to use externally. If you have consulted your planning officer and taken on board their recommendations, you stand a better chance of coming up with a scheme that will meet with the necessary approval.

Some authorities are inherently conservative and are concerned that new houses blend in as far as possible with the existing housing stock in terms of materials and architectural style. If you want to build a modern house in glass and steel in the middle of a conservation area where the houses are brick-built and Victorian, you may well encounter resistance. Do not despair if you meet with initial opposition. In many cases, a planner's reservations can be accommodated fairly painlessly by making minor changes to material specifications or elevational detail. Sometimes, you might even find that a planning officer will be intrigued by your proposals and prepared to champion your cause.

The planning process allows time for objections to be made. Do not assume that your proposals will slip unnoticed under the local radar. In many cases, it is best to be pro-active and involve your neighbours from the outset. Explain what you are trying to do and show them your plans. If your scheme has been properly considered and designed, they should have no solid grounds for objection. If your new house will come within a specified distance of the boundary with a neighbour's property – which may well be the case if it is a tight urban infill – you will also need a party wall award.

In the United States and other parts of the world, the process is broadly similar. Zoning ordinances specify which areas can be used for which purposes. Where land is zoned for residential use, there will be further stipulations and restrictions, governing how high you can build and how close to the street or other properties. In addition, there may also be guidelines on style and material use.

In order to build on a plot of land, you (or your architect or contractor) need to apply for a building permit. Depending on your proposals, this may be forwarded for zoning review. If there is an aspect of your scheme that flies in the face of local ordinances, you will either be asked to modify your plans or allowed to apply for a 'variance'.

Building regulations and codes

Building regulations or codes set the minimum standards for all new construction. They vary from area to area, but are chiefly concerned that what you build does not pose a hazard to you or to anyone else. In Britain, building regulations cover the design and construction of the basic structure, including foundations and drainage, as well as insulation, damp-proofing, ventilation, fire protection and means of escape. These regulations are detailed, specifying, for example, that all stairs must have handrails and all window-less bathrooms mechanical extract.

Building-control officers inspect initial plans, and subsequently pay a number of site visits to check work in progress. You need to take account of these inspections in your scheduling. If an inspector shows up to check that drains have been correctly laid and they have been covered with concrete, he or she has the right to insist that the concrete is dug up at your expense so the inspection can be carried out. Building regulations approval is granted once all necessary inspections have been passed satisfactorily.

If you have employed an architect or professional designer and are using a standard structural system, there is no reason your new house should not comply. Some self-builders, especially those attracted by the ecological possibilities of building out of adobe or straw bales, will find themselves with more of a fight on their hands. It is not unknown for eco designers to have had to campaign to change local codes or building regulations before proceeding with their plans.

The situation is broadly similar in the United States and other parts of the world. Codes may also set out requirements for plumbing, electrical systems, heating, ventilation and air conditioning. In the United States, after a building permit has been obtained, construction work will be inspected at a number of key stages to establish that it complies with local codes. If each stage passes approval, you will then receive a certificate of occupancy, which gives you the legal right to live in your house. This document is essential if you later decide to sell or if you should need to make an insurance claim.

DESIGN AND CONSTRUCTION OPTIONS

You have come up with a basic brief, put the financing in place and found a site. You may even have bought it. So where do you go from here? When it comes to the process of design and construction, there are a number of routes open. At one extreme, you might put your entire project in the hands of an architect or package-deal company, sit back and oversee the work from the sidelines. At the other, you may be literally raising the roof yourself with minimum professional support. In between are multiple options which require your involvement to a greater or lesser extent.

Architectural services

Many people fight shy of working with architects because of the common perception that they are expensive and domineering. That is far from the case. A good architect with experience in the self-build sector should be able to save you money, savings that might even offset the cost of their fees. While it is true that architects tend to have strong design preferences – that is why they are in the profession in the first place – it is up to you to find a practice with an approach that is compatible with your own. If you start off on the same wavelength, there should be no need for massive design clashes later. Similarly, costs spiral out of control when clients do not make it crystal clear how much they can spend. Do not be vague about money, either at the outset or at any stage thereafter.

Unless you opt for a package deal, you will almost be guaranteed to need architectural input at the initial design stage, if only to realize your scheme on paper and come up with a structural solution that can actually be built. A full architectural service will give you much more:

Advice on the purchase of land and planning issues Architects who have previously worked in the area will have dealt with the planning officers before and will know their preferences and sticking points – if not, they will waste no time opening the channels of communication. They might also have ongoing relationships with local estate agents or realtors, and be aware of possible sites coming on to the market.

Refinement of your requirements An initial consultation, which may be free of charge, can help to reconcile any discrepancies in your brief and put some firm parameters in place.

Assessment of potential Architects read sites the way other people read books. They will be able to point out assets and drawbacks that might not otherwise have occurred to you. They will also be able to advise you whether you need additional information such as site surveys or soil investigations.

Design An architect will develop a scheme design from initial sketch proposals right up to detailed drawings suitable for submission to the planning department, coming up with a solution that best satisfies your needs and budget, the specific nature of your site and the planners' likely response to the proposals.

Planning permission and building regulations An architect will negotiate all stages involved in gaining planning consent and building regulations approval. If there are any unusual site conditions or structural elements that need to be considered, your architect will commission a structural engineer or similar professional to come up with detail designs and calculations (at your expense).

Full specification and working drawings The next stage in the process is the production of working drawings to serve as a blueprint for the builder, along with a detailed specification of all works, materials, fixtures and fittings.

Choice of contractor The architect will put the scheme out for tender, sending plans and specifications to a shortlist of contractors, inviting quotations. Once the contractor has been selected, the architect will oversee the preparation of necessary contract documentation.

Site supervision The architect will liaise closely with the contractor and any subcontractors to ensure work progresses smoothly, to the agreed standard, and on schedule.

Inspection of defects and handover After your house is completed, your architect will tour the site, noting any defects in the work that need to be put right by the builder.

From the above list, you will see that for a small percentage of the total contract sum (generally less than 6 per cent in Britain) you will gain access to a breadth of expertise from knowledge of legalities and planning issues to contract management and design itself. If you decide not to opt for the full service, you can always employ an architect to get you past the planning permission hurdle and come up with a detailed scheme that you can then put in the hands of a builder or use yourself to instruct a series of subcontractors. Or you may be able to negotiate a reduced fee scale by sourcing materials yourself and coordinating deliveries.

Kits and package deals

Many self-builders, particularly in the United States, opt for a package deal which combines a design service with the supply of all necessary materials. Some companies recommend suitable builders for the construction; others provide a full construction service, down to the fitting of internal fixtures and final finishes.

Most kit or package-deal companies use timber-frame structural systems, regardless of how the house will be eventually clad. As the elements must be prefabricated weeks before delivery, a substantial sum is required up front.

There are a wide range of designs from which to choose, but it is fair to say that in most cases house types will be fairly conventional – these companies have an enviable track record when it comes to satisfying local authorities simply because they do not stray too far from the straight and narrow, and because they make it their business to accommodate regional variations with respect to style and detail. Some companies will also undertake either to customize one of their house types to suit your needs or to translate your requirements into a one-off design that is most likely to meet planning criteria.

Builders and subcontractors

Once your scheme has been designed and approved, you need to get it built. It is important to understand at the outset the difference between a builder (also known as a main or general contractor) and a subcontractor.

A builder organizes all work on site, manages and, if necessary, hires tradespeople and any plant, orders materials, coordinates deliveries and schedules inspections. A subcontractor is a specialist, such as a plumber, electrician or carpenter, who carries out a particular job on the build, and who may also supply the relevant materials and fixtures.

When it comes to construction there are a number of choices open to you. You can enter into a contract with a builder or building firm who will oversee the entire project from start to finish. Or you can engage a builder to complete the basic shell of your house to the point where it is watertight, then hire the necessary subcontractors to complete the job. Finally, you can choose to work directly with subcontractors right from the start of the project, taking on the managerial role yourself, along with as much of the labour as you are capable of doing.

There are pros and cons to each option. Generally, although not always, the more of the work that you do yourself, both managerial and hands-on, the cheaper the build will be. At the same time, you will be more exposed. If you hire a builder or building firm, you enter into a formal contractual relationship which gives you protection and redress if things go wrong. If you hire subcontractors directly, formal documentation is likely to be limited to either a letter of agreement or a quotation and schedule on headed paper, which will not be sufficient to cover you in the case of unforeseen expenses or events. Any problems that arise or additional costs will be your direct responsibility. In addition, some subcontractors only supply their labour, which means it is down to you to arrange not only for materials to be delivered on time, but also for any necessary tools or plant, such as mixers or diggers.

WORKING WITH PROFESSIONALS

Tracking down the right professional for the job is key in achieving a successful outcome. It is not simply a case of making sure that the person you employ has the relevant experience, although this is a good starting point. In many cases, but particularly when it comes to design professionals, it is also important to establish that they are on your wavelength and know what you are trying to achieve. This ensures that lines of communication remain open as the work progresses. A healthy creative dialogue is one thing, but head-to-head clashes over every detail quite another.

When you employ someone in whatever capacity, you are necessarily entering into a relationship, albeit a commercial one. Except in rare cases, or for very straightforward jobs, this relationship is more complicated than other forms of business transaction, such as handing over money at a cash register in exchange for a product. If you have done your homework and researched the market properly to find the right person or company, it does not end with your signature at the bottom of the contract or letter of agreement. Working with professionals means engaging in a process where there is trust and respect on both sides. Clients who are unreasonably suspicious, fault-find to the nth degree and impose intolerable conditions on working practices, and who are not prepared to compromise when work is held up by unforeseen hitches, are less likely to achieve what they want in the long run, no matter who they employ, than those who take a more realistic and adaptable approach.

Research the market

Finding the right professional is a similar process whether you are employing a painter-decorator or an architect, seeking the advice of a surveyor or hiring a plumber. Research may take a while, but you should think of this stage as a necessary period of preparation which has the potential to save you hard-earned money, as well as time and distress.

Start looking around for the people to do the job well in advance of your planned start date. You will find that the best ones are usually booked up for some time into the future.

Ask for personal recommendations, from architects, from package-deal companies and from other self-builders. People love to talk about their building projects and will be happy to share their experiences with you, both the successes and the disasters. You will get an insider's view on what it is like to deal with a particular company or professional, and a more honest assessment than more formal references often provide.

Trade magazines, local newspapers and the Internet may help you to locate suitable professionals in your area. Keep a weather eye out for articles that feature the type of work you intend to commission.

Professional or accredited trade organizations generally maintain a register of their members that can also help to direct you to a local company or service. Membership of one of these bodies indicates that a level of competence and appropriate training has been passed.

Draw up a shortlist of at least three different companies. This approach is not necessary for a straightforward plumbing or electrical job, but it will give you a broader picture of cost and scheduling options if you are engaging a contractor or design practice.

If employing design professionals, ask to see their portfolio and, if possible, arrange to visit a completed scheme. Both architects and interior designers generally have some sort of stylistic signature; it is rare to find very different approaches within the same portfolio. If you want a modern look, it is no use approaching someone with a more traditional bent and expecting to see eye to eye over a proposed scheme.

Ask for three references from each company or person on your shortlist and take them up.

Word of mouth

Ask the following questions when seeking personal recommendations. Did the contractor or professional:

+ turn up on time at the agreed hour in the morning?
+ turn up every day until all of the work was completed?
+ carry out the work to the agreed standard and specification?
+ maintain safe and well-organized work conditions?
+ clean up the work site at the end of the day to a reasonable standard?
+ possess the appropriate qualifications or levels of training?
+ carry liability insurance?
+ keep you informed about progress and any unforeseen hitches?

Making comparisons

Once you have narrowed your choice down to a likely shortlist, the next stage is to ask for an estimate of how much the work will cost and how long it will take to complete. You stand a far better chance of gaining a realistic picture if you can be as specific as possible about your requirements. A thorough, itemized brief which spells out the type of materials, fixtures and finishes you want will save delays, misunderstandings and disappointments at a later date and will allow specific price comparisons to be made.

If you are shopping around for ideas as well as for skills and professional advice, be prepared to explore the options creatively with your designer or architect. You may wish to approach several companies or practitioners with a view to commissioning an outline scheme to form the basis of a more detailed brief. Then you can proceed with the one that matches your expectations and budget most closely, and draw up a brief on that basis.

When it comes to planning a project, cost is one of the principal determining factors. Everyone likes to get value for money; no one wants to pay more than necessary. But because money is such an issue, you need to be clear-sighted about what the work ought to cost so you are not tempted either by false economies or by companies that come in with suspiciously low estimates.

Drawing up contracts

The purpose of a contract is to spell out the services, materials and work you are entitled to expect for your money, and when. Just as important, however, it should provide a means of redress should things go wrong. A contract should not simply cover what you expect to happen; it should also indicate how problems can be resolved when the unexpected happens. Many disputes arise when specifications or plans are changed somewhere down the line. The extra costs that these changes incur can sometimes be avoided, but not always, and you will need to be sure of your position.

If you are employing an architect, he or she will draw up the formal contract with your builder for you. Alternatively, you might wish to engage the services of a solicitor. Many self-builders use standard short contracts which are widely available, cover all the contingencies and are written in plain and simple terms.

Subcontractors tend to be hired on the basis of a letter of agreement, or quotation and time estimate, set out on headed paper. This is still a legal document, although it does not provide you with the same rights of redress as a full contract with a builder should any problems arise.

Payment

The contract or letter of agreement should set out in detail all payment arrangements, including when stage payments should be made and the percentage to be retained upon completion in case of defects, which is normally a sum in the region of 5 per cent of the contract value.

Never pay up front and be suspicious of entering into any arrangement with a builder who requests a hefty advance. Make sure that the stage payments are spaced so that the builder or subcontractor has enough incentive to finish the work. In most cases, if you are hiring a subcontractor directly, it is best to insist on the quotation of a fixed rate for the job. Day rates give subcontractors the perfect excuse to spin out the work unnecessarily (and expensively).

How to avoid problems

The best way to avoid problems is to hire the right people in the first place. Do your homework, follow up references and recommendations, and make sure you are absolutely satisfied that a firm or individual has the right professional qualifications and insurances.

Once the build is under way, problems can be prevented, or their effects minimized, if you maintain a good working relationship with those you have engaged to work on the build. Again, it is important that you do your homework. Just because you won't be laying the drains yourself, it does not mean you shouldn't bother to inform yourself about the basic procedures, materials and regulations involved. All self-builders find themselves on a learning curve – make sure that yours is not too steep. The more you know about what is happening and what it is that needs to happen next, the more informed your dialogue with the professionals involved will be. Learn the sequence of work so you do not have unrealistic expectations.

Be courteous in your dealings with those you employ. Thanks to scare stories in the press and television programmes that rely on tales of disaster and woe for their viewing figures, many people are naturally suspicious of anyone who is remotely connected with the building industry. Once you have established that you have hired the best person or firm for the job, put any feelings of suspicion aside and treat those who are working for you with respect.

Keep the lines of communication open. Agree set times for inspection and allow enough time for proper consultation. If you have made yourself unavailable when a decision needs to be made, you may find you do not agree with the result when it is too late to do anything about it. At the same time, resist the temptation to stick your oar in at every opportunity. Professionals do not like being told how to do their job, and no one likes to work with someone hovering anxiously over their shoulder asking distracting questions.

Do not keep changing your mind about finishes, materials, fixtures and fittings. When building projects run massively over budget, it is often because self-builders get carried away and up the specification at every turn. Keep an eye on your budget at every stage of the game. If you do conceive a sudden desire for marble tiles in the bathroom, make sure you cover the additional cost by making a saving somewhere else. All 'extras' or changes to the specification should be agreed in writing.

Maintain a safe and tidy site. If you are hiring subcontractors directly, site maintenance may be a useful role for you to take on. See Safety on page 169 for essential guidelines.

Expect the unexpected. All building projects turn up something out of the ordinary. You might find that a supplier cannot provide a particular material, fitting or fixture that you have ordered; you may run into a patch of particularly bad weather; you may discover very different ground conditions than the soil survey had led you to expect. When a problem arises, the important thing is not to panic and to keep an open mind. If a material is unavailable, research an alternative – it might prove better and even cheaper in the long run. If you face additional expense due to an unforeseen ground, servicing or structural problem, remind yourself that is why you have purposely built in a contingency allowance.

If you do find yourself in a dispute with your builder, subcontractor or supplier, try to be as objective as possible. Resist the temptation to wade in and assign blame left, right and centre before you are in full possession of the facts. Put your complaints down on paper, arrange a meeting to talk it through and see if you can find a way forward. In severe cases, where there is obvious bad workmanship or long periods of inactivity on site, it is time to fall back on the contract and consult your solicitor, or to fire the subcontractor who has proved not up to the job.

Finally, ease the pressure both on yourself and the rest of your family by making sensible and comfortable living arrangements for the period of the build. If you are able to remain in your existing house, that is all well and good. Many self-builders, however, need to sell their previous property to finance the build. Some self-builders are happy in a caravan or mobile home on site, but that is not practical for most families. Keep family life ticking over as best you can to prevent the build-up of stress – self-build is absorbing, perhaps even a little obsessional, but do not let it take over your life to the detriment of your career and relationships.

SAFETY

There is no such thing as taking site safety too seriously. A building site presents literally hundreds of hazards. Self-builders are even more at risk than professionals or construction workers, who have a better familiarity with the potential dangers. Just to take one example, many people do not realize that concrete and mortar and cement dust can cause serious burns to unprotected skin if not washed off immediately and thoroughly.

- Wear the right protective clothing. That includes hard hat, thick-soled boots, gloves for working with chemicals, cement or mortar, ear protectors for working with noisy machinery and goggles for working with saws or grinders. Insist that everyone on site wears protective gear, including visitors. Always keep a well-equipped first-aid box on site for minor cuts and scrapes.
- Keep the site tidy and well organized. Accidents are less likely to happen if there are no stray materials or tools lying around.
- Ensure that electric equipment has an appropriate circuit breaker or safety cut-off. Make sure you obtain and read safety manuals.
- Keep toxic chemicals and petrol under lock and key.
- Make sure that all supplies and materials are stacked in low, stable piles so there is no risking of them toppling over.
- Guard against falls. Secure ladders top and bottom. Do not be tempted to walk on unfixed joists or joists that are not covered by temporary boarding. Fix up a rope or timber balustrade to prevent yourself falling down a stairwell. Exercise great caution on roofs.
- Be very cautious when working in deep trenches or any other site excavations. Always work with other people when you are engaged in deep excavation.
- Be aware of your limitations. If you are not used to heavy labour, you run a real risk of back injury or muscle strain if you push yourself beyond what you are physically capable of.
- A building site is no place for children (even the best behaved) or pets.

THE SEQUENCE OF WORK

Much of the success of your building project will depend on making sure the right procedures are carried out at the right time, so it is vital to make yourself familiar with the sequence of work, if only to keep expectations realistic. If you are managing the site yourself, keeping on schedule is every bit as important as sticking to your budget. Jumping the gun can be just as bad as falling behind. Materials, fixtures or fittings that are ordered too early will sit around on site, getting in the way, and may be damaged, lost or stolen. Rushing through work before official inspections is potentially disastrous.

From the moment the ground is first broken to when the last slate is nailed on the roof, the rush will be on to get the basic shell up and watertight. This is the crunch time for self-build. Once the structure is up and the roof is on, you can be more relaxed about timing.

1. Permissions, applications and warranties

Planning permission must be in place before you start, as should insurance and warranties. It is also advisable to apply to the gas, water and electric utilities well before your start date to allow for the necessary notice periods. You will also need to have arranged site access, site security and storage for materials and tools.

2. Demolition and site preparation

The very first work on site will be preparation of the ground: demolishing any unwanted structures, clearing away garbage and junk, removing trees (if permitted), clearing topsoil for later use and levelling the ground.

3. Excavations

Your architect or builder will already have specified the type of foundations you require, depending on the ground conditions and the structural system that you are employing. At this stage, excavations for foundations and service trenches will be dug and a base laid down for paths, driveways and patios. Even when a full soil survey has been carried out, actual conditions may turn out to be different from what was expected, in which case different foundations will have to be allowed for. Bad weather can also delay progress.

4. Foundations

The next stage is to pour the foundation concrete – again, this is a time when you should keep an eye on the weather. Note: This is an inspection stage.

5. The damp-proof course and foundation brickwork or blockwork

Once the foundation concrete is laid, brick or block walls are built up to ground level and the dpc (damp-proof course) is laid.
Note: This is an inspection stage.

6. Ground floor construction

There are different types of ground-floor structure: concrete slab, beam and block, and suspended timber. Whichever one is employed, once this 'oversite' stage is completed, the shell can start to go up.
Note: This is an inspection stage.

7. The shell or superstructure

What happens next depends on the type of structural system that you are employing. If you have opted for a kit with extensive prefabricated elements, the shell may go up in a flash. Similarly, timber-frame structures tend to be erected more quickly than those which are made of brick or block – such construction is more labour-intensive, and more likely to get held up by bad weather. Once the roof structure is covered and any external cladding is in place, the shell is complete and the most hectic period is over. Depending on the type of structure being built, a number of warranty inspections will need to be carried out at different stages of the shell's construction (and after first-fix). Before the scaffolding is taken down, both the guttering and flashings should also be fixed, along with any vent pipes.

8. First-fix carpentry

This stage includes work on door and window frames and the installation of external doors.

9. Drains

Pipework for drains and services are laid and brought into the shell. Trenches must not be covered up until the work has been inspected and any drains tested.
Note: This is an inspection stage.

10. Filling in drainage and service trenches

Once the drains have been tested, all trenches can be filled.

11. Glazing windows

Glazing windows makes the house fully waterproof.

12. Internal construction and first-fix

Load-bearing internal walls will have been put in place during the erection of the shell. Now partitions and staircases can be constructed. This is also the stage for first-fix plumbing and electrical work, such as the laying of pipework and routing of wiring. Insulation is installed, and walls are covered with plaster or plasterboard.

13. Second-fix and fitting out

Once the walls have been plastered or boarded, the plumber returns to fit the sanitaryware and sinks. The electrician returns to fit switches, lights and other electrical fixtures. Power and water are now on. The carpenter's second fix includes internal doors, mouldings, skirting (baseboards), the construction of built-in cupboards and the construction or installing of kitchen units.

14. Decoration

Paint or other wall finishes, including tiling, are applied. Final floors are laid.

15. Final inspection and handover

The building inspector and warranty inspector make their final visit to the site. The architect inspects the house for any defects.

Architects featured in the case studies

pages 20–5
Bercy Chen Studio LLP
2844 Shoalcrest Avenue
Austin, TX 78705
USA
T: +1 512 481 0092
F: +1 512 476 7664
www.bcarc.com

pages 26–31
Fung + Blatt Architects
104 North Avenue 56
Suite 3A
Los Angeles, CA 90042
USA
T: +1 323 255 8368
F: +1 323 255 3646
www.fungandblatt.com

pages 32–7
Smith Caradoc-Hodgkins
Architects Ltd
43 Tanner Street
London SE1 3PL
UK
T: +44 (0)20 7407 0171
F: +44 (0)20 7407 0792
www.sch-architects.com

pages 38–43
McIntosh Poris
Associates
36801 Woodward Avenue
Suite 200
Birmingham, MI 48009
USA
T: +1 248 258 9346
F: +1 248 258 0967
www.mcintoshporis.com

pages 44–9
Sander Architects
310 Washington Bld, #109
Marina del Rey, CA 90202
USA
T: +1 310 822 0300
F: +1 310 822 0900
www.sander-architects.com

pages 50–5
Robert Dye Associates
Linton House
39–51 Highgate Road
London NW5 1RS
UK
T: +44 (0)20 7267 9388
F: +44 (0)20 7267 9345

pages 58–63
blocdesign
5 Eurella Street
Kenmore 4069
Queensland
Australia
T: +61 7 3720 2342
F: +61 7 3720 3241
www.blocdcl.com

pages 64–71
Roderick James
Architects LLP
Seagull House
Dittisham Mill Creek
Dartmouth
Devon TQ6 0HZ
UK
T: +44 (0)1803 722 472
F: +44 (0)1803 722 472
www.roderickjames
architects.com

Carpenter Oak Limited
The Framing Yard
East Cornworthy
Totnes
Devon TQ9 7HF
UK
T: +44 (0)1803 732 900
F: +44 (0)1803 732 901
www.carpenteroak.com

pages 72–9
John Pardey Architects
Beck Farm Studio
St Leonard's Road
East End
Lymington
Hampshire SO41 5SR
UK
T: +44 (0)1590 626 465
F: +44 (0)1590 626 547
www.johnpardey
architects.com

pages 80–5
Hillery Priest
Architecture Ltd
128 Ponsonby Road
Auckland
New Zealand
T: +64 9 376 6337
F: +64 9 376 6442
www.hillerypriest.co.nz

pages 86–91
AV62 Arquitectos SL
Girona 62
Bajos Derecha
Barcelona 08009
Spain
T: +34 93 231 2266
F: + 34 93 231 3734
www.av62arquitectos.com

pages 92–97
Super E
T: 00 800 3999 9969 (free phone inside the UK)
T: +1 519 539 9762 (outside the UK)
www.super-e.com

UK Super E member:
DGS construction
T: +44 (0)1908 503 147
www.dgsconstruction.co.uk

Canadian Super E member:
DAC International
T: +1 613 839 0888
F: +1 613 839 0939
www.dac.ca

pages 98–103
Soeters Van Eldonk
Ponec Architecten
Kerkstraat 204
1017 GV Amsterdam
The Netherlands
T: +44 20 624 2939
F: +44 20 624 6928
www.soetersvaneldonk
ponec.nl

pages 104–9
Green Yard Architecture
226 College Road
Norwich
Norfolk NR2 3JA
UK
T: +44 (0)1603 455 844
F: +44 (0)1603 455 633

INDEX

174

INDEX

USEFUL CONTACTS

Advice and organizations

American Institute of Architects
T: +1 800 365 ARCH
www.aiaaccess.com
Directory of architects in the US

The American Institute of
Building Design
T: +1 800 366 2423
www.aibd.org
Standard and code of ethics

Association for Environment-
Conscious Building (AECB)
T: +44 (0)1559 370 908
www.aecb.net
Advice on sustainable building

Better Business Bureau
www.bbb.org/library/home-imp.asp
Information on planning,
financing, hiring contractors, etc

BuilderDirectory.com
www.builderdirectory.com
Guide to architects, builders
and engineers across the US

The Building Centre Group
T: +44 (0)9065 161 136
www.buildingcentre.co.uk
Advice and information on
construction and materials

Building Research
Establishment (BRE)
T: +44 (0)1923 664 000
www.bre.co.uk
Advice on environmentally aware
building; materials exchange

Centre for Alternative Technology
T: +44 (0) 1654 703 409
www.cat.org.uk
Information on all aspects of
alternative technology

Conservation and Renewable
Energy Inquiry and Referral
Service (CAREIRS)
T: +1 800 523 2929
Information on wind power, solar
heating and photovoltaics

Construction Resources
T: +44 (0)20 7450 2211
www.constructionresources.com
Information on ecological building

Council for Registered Gas
Installers (CORGI)
T: +44 (0)1256 372 200
www.corgi-gas.com
Registers all gas-installation
businesses

Efficient Windows Collaborative
T: +1 202 857 0666
www.efficientwindows.org
High-efficiency windows & doors

Electrical Contractors' Association
T: +44 (0)20 7313 4800
www.eca.co.uk
Information; index of members

Energy Saving Trust
T: +44 (0)20 7222 0101
www.est.org.uk
Information on energy efficiency

Environmental Building News
T: +1 802 257 7300
www.BuildingGreen.com
Publications on eco building

Federation of Master Builders
T: +44 (0)20 7242 7583
www.fmb.org.uk
Contact for an index of members

Forest Stewardship Council: UK
T: +44 (0)1686 431 916
www.fsc-uk.org
Forest Stewardship Council: US
T: +1 877 372 5646
www.fscus.org
Sets standards for timber
management and products

Institute of Carpenters
T: +44 (0)115 949 0641
www.central-office.co.uk
Information and index of members

Institute of Plumbing
T: +44 (0)1708 472 791
www.plumbers.org.uk
Index of members

Institute of Structural Engineers
T: +44 (0)20 7235 4535
www.istructe.org.uk
www.findanengineer.com
Index of members

National Association of Home
Builders (NAHB)

T: +1 800 368 5242
www.nahb.org
Information and advice

National Association of Realtors
T: +1 202 383 1000
www.nar.realtor.com
Education service for self-builders

National House Building Council
T: +44 (0)1494 735 363
www.nhbc.co.uk
Register of new houses

Plumbing Heating Cooling
Contractors National
Association (PHCC)
T: +1 800 533 7694
www.phccweb.org
Professional referral service

Royal Institute of British
Architects
T: +44 (0)20 7580 5533
www.riba.org
Contact for a list of members

Royal Institute of Chartered
Surveyors
T: +44 (0)870 333 1600
www.rics.org.uk
Contact for a list of members

Solar Energy Industries
Association
T: +1 202 628 7745
www.seia.org
American trade association of
companies offering solar products

Finding sites

On-line site-finding services
may require a subscription. In
the US, vacant lots are generally
offered through realtors.

Landbank Services
T: +44 (0)118 962 6022
www.landbank.co.uk

Plotfinder
T: +44 (0)906 557 5400
www.plotfinder.net

Plotsearch
T: +44 (0)870 870 9004
www.buildstore.co.uk/plotsearch

Prefab and kit houses

Apropos
T: +44 (0) 8000 328 0033

gd@clearspan.co.uk
Bespoke glass structures

Custom Homes
T: +44 (0)1787 377 388
www.customhomes.co.uk
Largest package-deal company
in Britain

Glidehouse
www.livemodern.com/glidehouse
Cutting-edge modular homes

Huf Haus
T: +44 (0)1932 828 502
www.huf-haus.com
Award-winning post-and-beam
kit houses from Germany

LOT-EK
T: +1 212 255 9326
www.lot-ek.com
Container home kits

Potton Ltd
T: +44 (0)1480 401 401
www.potton.co.uk
Large British package-deal
company catering for the more
traditional end of the market

Oakmasters
T: +44 (0)1444 455 455
www.oakmasters.co.uk
Bespoke oak-frame buildings

weeHouse
T: +1 651 647 6650
www.weehouses.com
Prefab modules that arrive ready
to live in. Currently available in
Midwest and West Coast states.

Salvage

American Salvage
T: +1 305 836 4444
www.americansalvage.com

Architectural Salvage Register
T: +44 (0)1483 203 221
Register of architectural
materials suppliers

LASSco
T: +44 (0)20 7749 9944
Long-established and
comprehensive salvage

Whole House Building Supply
T: +1 650 856 0634
Freephone: +1 800 364 0634
www.driftwoodsalvage.com

Photographic Acknowledgments

The publisher would like to thank the following photographers, agencies and architects for their kind permission to reproduce the following photographs in this book:

Endpapers Annabel Elston; 2 Sean Laurenz/House & Leisure/Photozest/ Inside (Designed and built by Bruce Attwood); 4–5 Denise Prince Martin (Architect: Bercy Chen Studio); 6–7 Alan Weintraub/Arcaid (Architect: Lautner Associates); 7 above Richard Powers; 7 below Helen Binet/Arcblue (Architect: David Chipperfield); 9 above Ray Main/Mainstream (Architect: Chris Cowper); 9 centre Huf Haus; 9 below left Guy Obijn (Architect: Philip Mortelmans); 9 below right Richard Glover/View (Architect: Ellen Woolley); 10 Undine Prohl (Architect: Safdie/Rabines); 12 Mark Luscombe-Whyte/The Interior Archive (Architect: Robert Dye); 13 Sharon Risedorph (Architect: Sander Architects); 14–15 Sue Barr/View (Architect: Robert Doe); 16 Courtesy of Robert Doe; 17 Peter Cook/View (Architect: Robert Doe); 18 above left Courtesy of Robert Doe; 18 above right Peter Cook/View (Architect: Robert Doe); 18 below Sue Barr/View (Architect: Robert Doe); 19 Peter Cook/View (Architect: Robert Doe); 20–1 Denise Prince Martin (Architect: Bercy Chen Studio); 22 left Mike Osborne (Architect: Bercy Chen Studio); 22, 23 and 24–5 Denise Prince Martin (Architect: Bercy Chen Studio); 25 Mike Osborne (Architect: Bercy Chen Studio); 26–7 Richard Powers (Architect: Fung + Blatt); 28 Courtesy of Fung + Blatt Architects; 29–31 below Richard Powers (Architect: Fung + Blatt); 32–7 Darren Chung (Architect: Smith Caradoc Hodgkins); 38–9 Juliana Sohn/MS Logan Ltd (Architect: McIntosh Poris Associates); 40 Courtesy McIntosh Poris Associates; 41 Juliana Sohn/ MS Logan Ltd (Architect: McIntosh Poris Associates); 42 Balthazar Korab/Courtesy McIntosh Poris Associates; 42–3 and 43 below left Juliana Sohn/MS Logan Ltd (Architect: McIntosh Poris Associates); 43 below right Balthazar Korab/Courtesy McIntosh Poris Associates; 44–5 Sharon Risedorph (Architect: Sander Architects); 46 Courtesy of Sander Architects; 47–9 Sharon Risedorph (Architect: Sander Architects); 50–5 Mark Luscombe-Whyte/The Interior

Archive (Architect: Robert Dye); 56 Richard Powers (Architect: bloc design); 57 Annabel Elston; 58 David Sandison (Architect: bloc design); 59–63 Richard Powers (Architect: bloc design); 64–71 Annabel Elston (Architect: Roderick James Architects); 72–3 James Morris (Architect: John Pardey Architects); 74 and 74–5 centre Courtesy of John Pardey Architects; 75 James Morris (Architect: John Pardey Architects); 76 above Courtesy of John Pardey Architects; 77–9 below James Morris (Architect: John Pardey Architects); 80–1 Nathalie Krag/Taverne Agency/ Stylist: Tami Christiansen (Architect: Hillery Priest Architecture Ltd); 82 above Courtesy of Hillery Priest Architecture Ltd; 82 below and 83–5 Nathalie Krag/Taverne Agency/Stylist: Tami Christiansen (Architect: Hillery Priest Architecture Ltd); 86–7 Eugeni Pons/RBA (Architect: AV62 Arquitectos); 88 Courtesy of AV62 Arquitectos; 89, 90 above left and above right Eugeni Pons/RBA (Architect: AV62 Arquitectos); 90 below Courtesy of AV62 Arquitectos; 91 Eugeni Pons/RBA (Architect: AV62 Arquitectos); 92–7 Annabel Elston 2004 (Design and Manufacture: Super E®); 98–9 Scagliola/Brakkee (Architect: Soeters Van Eldonk Ponec architecten); 100 Courtesy of Soeters Van Eldonk Ponec architecten; 101–2 Scagliola/Brakkee (Architect: Soeters Ven Eldonk Ponec architecten); 103 above Courtesy of Soeters Van Eldonk Ponec architecten; 103 below Scagliola/Brakkee (Architect: Soeters Van Eldonk Ponec architecten); 104–5 Simon Upton/The Interior Archive (Architect: GreenYard Architecture); 106 GreenYard Architecture; 107 Simon Upton/The Interior Archive (Architect: GreenYard Architecture); 108 above GreenYard Architecture; 108 below Simon Upton/The Interior Archive (Architect: GreenYard Architecture); 109 above GreenYard Architecture; 109 below Simon Upton/The Interior Archive (Architect: GreenYard Architecture); 110–11 Mads Mogensen (Architect: Peter Wenger); 111 above Dennis Gilbert/View (Architect: Richard Horden Associates); 111 below Courtesy of Natural Space Domes; 112–13 Giorgio Possenti/Vega MG (Architect: Studio Internazionale); 114–15 Jean-Francois Jaussaud; 115 Richard Sprengler/Rocio Romero; 116 J J Sulin (Architects: John

Vetter and Kelly Denk); 117 above Courtesy of the Walker Art Center, Minneapolis; 117 below weeHouse (Architect: Geoffrey Warner); 118 Nigel Rigden; 120 left Ray Main/Mainstream (Architect: Alastair Howe); 120 right John Edward/Arcaid (Architect: Fernau & Hartman); 121 Paul Massey (Architect: Springett & Mackay); 122 Margherita Spiluttini (Architect: Herzog & de Meuron); 124 Richard Powers (Architect: Daniel Marshall); 125 Dennis Gilbert/View (Architect: O'Donnell & Tuomey); 126 Stefan Thurmann/Hauser/Picture Press (Architect: Herman & Valentiny); 127 Mads Mogensen (Architect: Peter Wenger); 128 Werner Huthmacher (Architect: Schultz & Partners); 129 Giulio Oriani/Vega MG (Architect: Anya van der Merwe); 130 Mark Luscombe-Whyte/The Interior Archive (Architect: Sarah Wigglesworth); 131 Mark Munro (Architect: Bellemocat); 132 Rauno Traskelin/Courtesy of Helin & co Architects; 134 Mark Luscombe-Whyte/The Interior Archive (Architect: Nicolas Tye); 135 Ray Main/Mainstream (Cob in Cornwall); 136 Richard Powers (Architect: bloc design); 137 Hotze Eisma/Taverne Agency; 138 left Eugeni Pons/Vega MG; 138 right Richard Powers (Architect: Alex Smith); 139 above Jefferson Smith/Arcblue (Architect: Knott Architects); 139 below Alan Weintraub/Arcaid (Architect: Rene Davids & Christine Killory); 140 Dennis Gilbert/View (Architect: Richard Horden Associates); 141 Richard Powers (Architect: bloc design); 143 Ray Main/Mainstream; 144–5 Friedrich Busam/Architekturphoto (Architect: Roberto Briccola); 146 Liam Frederick/ Courtesy of Rob Paulus Architect; 148 Courtesy of Jestico + Whiles and the Museum of Welsh Life; 149 Richard Powers (Architect: Andrew Lister); 150 Sean Laurenz/House & Leisure/ Photozest/Inside (Designed and built by Bruce Attwood); 151 Richard Powers (Architect: Isay Weinfeld); 152–3 Annabel Elston

Every effort has been made to trace the copyright holders. We apologize in advance for any unintentional omissions and would be pleased to insert the appropriate acknowledgment in any subsequent publication.

Author's Acknowledgments

I would like to thank Zia Mattocks, Liz Boyd, Carl Hodson, and all the team at Conran Octopus for all their dedicated work in putting this book together.

First published in 2005 by Conran Octopus Limited, a part of Octopus Publishing Group, 2–4 Heron Quays, London E14 4JP
www.conran-octopus.co.uk

Text copyright © Elizabeth Whilhide 2005
Design and layout copyright © Conran Octopus 2005

The right of Elizabeth Wilhide to be identified as Author of this Work has been asserted by her in accordance with the Copyright, Designs and Patents Act 1998

All rights reserved. No part of this work may be reproduced, stored in a retrieval system or transmitted in any form or by any means, electronic, electrostatic, magnetic tape, mechanical, photocopying, recording or otherwise, without prior permission in writing of the publisher.

Publishing Director: Lorraine Dickey
Executive Editor: Zia Mattocks
Picture Research Manager: Liz Boyd
Art Director: Jonathan Christie
Designer: Carl Hodson
Production Manager: Angela Couchman

British Cataloguing-in-Publication Data.
A catalogue record for this book is available from the British Library.

ISBN 1 84091 421 1

Printed and bound in China